# CONTRADICTIONS IN LIVING ENVIRONMENT:

## An analysis of 22 Spanish houses

# CONTRADICTIONS IN LIVING ENVIRONMENT:
## AN ANALYSIS OF 22 SPANISH HOUSES

David Mackay ARIBA

## CROSBY LOCKWOOD & SON LTD
### 26 OLD BROMPTON ROAD · LONDON · SW7

First published 1971

ISBN 0 258 96776 5

Printed in Great Britain

# PREFACE

The intention of this book is twofold. In the first place it is to illustrate a personal selection of houses built in Spain during the decade 1960—70 which I believe contribute to a critical interpretation of the living environment. The term *living environment* implies a built physical surrounding alive to the change and flux of life rather than the narrower term *environment* alone which to me indicates only the conditioning circumstances as found. What I have tried to do is to suggest that the paradoxes and conflicts of this more fluid response to the situation be accepted as contradictions which can be absorbed within architecture to give it a critical meaning, thus, in its turn, actively contributing itself to the living environment. The second intention grew out of the first in an attempt to capture in words my own critical approach to the selected houses. This second intention, which comes first in the order of the book as an introduction, suffers from an inherent failure in that it attempts too much for a mere introduction. There are far too many points which need either further explanation or deliberation, but in a way I hope that this will provoke the reader to imaginative speculation and imaginative criticism.

It can be seen therefore, that this double intention goes beyond the typology and geography of the selected building and its critical approach can be applied to architecture generally and internationally. This is just what I and my partners, Josep Ma Martorell and Oriol Bohigas, are doing in introducing this critical attitude to society into the fabric of schools, factories or housing groups, etc. The acute test remains, however, in the realm of the private home where the user is in direct contact with the architect.

The book is divided into two parts, the introduction, which suggests a different emphasis to architecture from the technological and methodological approach, and the twenty-two houses, which I selected because I was looking for what I liked, and from which, once selected, I could learn. The introduction does not tie up nicely with the selected houses — few theories do with reality. However, I have introduced some small illustrations, which together with their text, help to bridge the gap between this fragile, or soft, theory and the elusive reality.

Finally, this book would never have been written if my ideas had not been encouraged, in the first place, by Humphrey Wilson, who came to me through the good offices of our mutual friend, the former R.I.B.A. librarian James Palmes.

*Barcelona, February, 1971*                                                    DAVID MACKAY

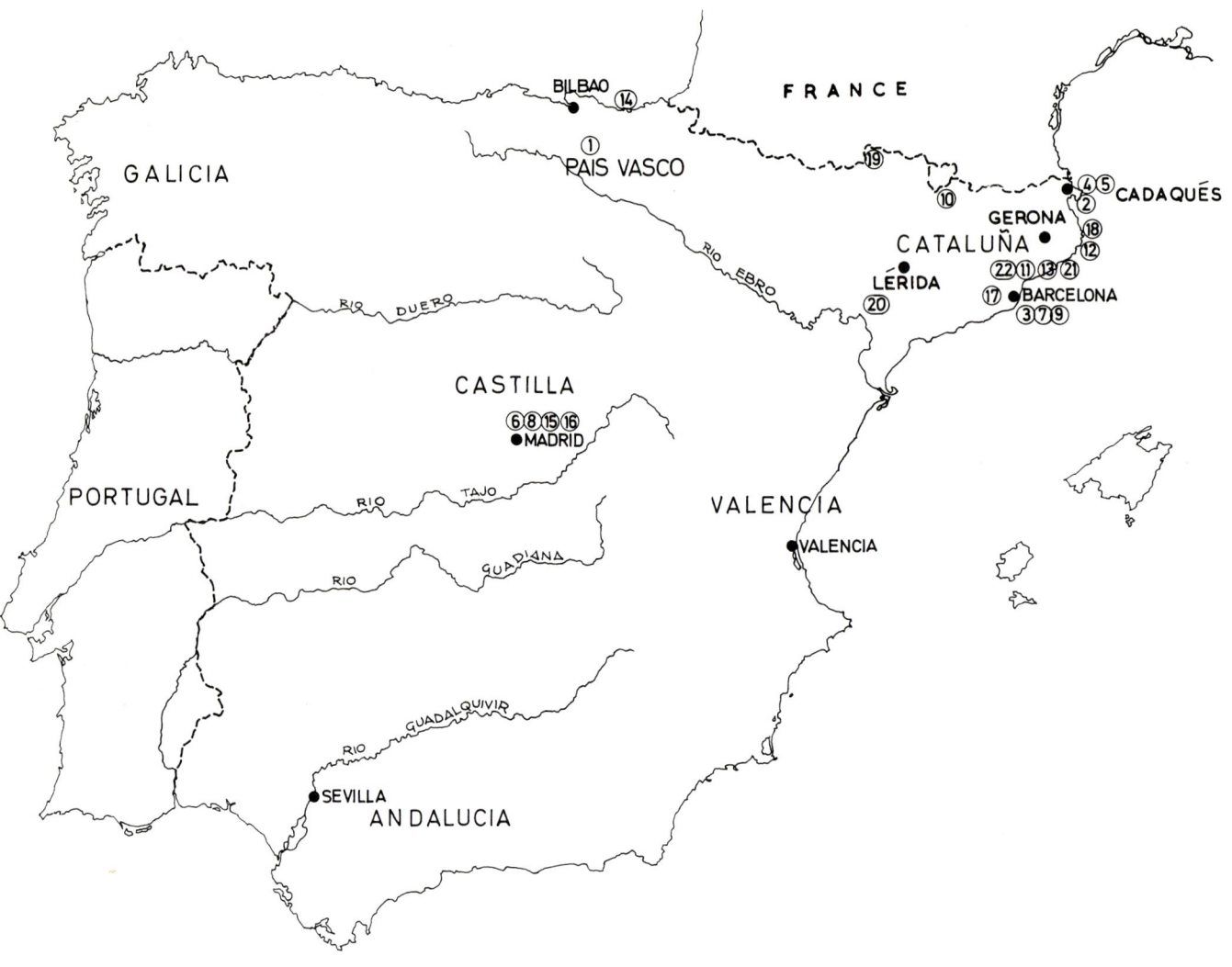

The numbers of the 22 houses which are
described and analysed in the text are shown on
the map above.

# CONTENTS

## PHOTO CREDITS

# CUTTINGS

"The detached house of moderate size . . . made its appearance as the dwelling of the yeoman when economic conditions in late medieval England encouraged the rise of a class between the feudal landowner and the peasant parallel to the skilled artisan class in the towns. . . . Around 1800 the newly fashionable attitude gave prestige to modest detached dwellings, raising the social status of the 'cottage' from an agricultural labourer's hovel to a middle-class habitation, or even on occasion a holiday 'retreat' for the upper-classes — at first by adding the French adjective *orné*. At the same time the status of the 'villa' tended to be reduced from a large Italianate mansion on its own estate to a moderate-sized house at the edge of town".
HENRY RUSSELL HITCHCOCK
(*Architecture: Nineteenth and Twentieth Centuries.* Penguin Books p. 253)

"The house of moderate cost is not only (a country's) major architectural problem but the problem most difficult for her major architects".
FRANK LLOYD WRIGHT
(*The Natural House.* Mentor Books p. 68)

"The problem of the house is a problem of the epoch. The equilibrium of society today depends on it. Architecture has for its first duty, in this period of renewal, that of bringing about a revision of values, a revision of the constituent elements of the house".
LE CORBUSIER
(*Towards a New Architecture.* Architectural Press p. 210)

". . . the chief obstacle to any real solution of the moderate-cost house problem is the fact that our people do not really know how to live. They imagine their idiosyncrasies to be their 'tastes', their prejudices to be their predilections, and their ignorance to be virtue where any beauty of living is concerned".
FRANK LLOYD WRIGHT
(*The Natural House.* Mentor Books p. 68)

"Everybody, quite rightly, dreams of sheltering himself in a sure and permanent home of his own . . . when the time does arrive for building this house, it is not the mason's nor the craftsman's moment, but that moment in which every man makes ONE poem, at any rate, in his life. And so, in our towns and their outskirts, we have had during the last forty years not so much houses as POEMS, poems of an Indian summer, . . . ."
LE CORBUSIER
(*Towards a New Architecture.* Architectural Press p. 245)

# INTRODUCTION

## 1. TOWARDS A DEFINITION OF THE OTHER SIDE OF ARCHITECTURE

### SUMMARY
There are two sides of architecture—the verbal (interpretation) and the formal (creation)—both of which reflect the crisis of ethos, due to the breakdown of the geographical and social boundaries, which is leading pluralist societies to a more universal sensitive inter-dependence and a search for new concrete definitions.

The apparent fragmentation of mental attitudes is due to the rejection of reality which alone gives the clue to a converging praxis. As reality responds to the fluidity of the situation, it escapes complete definition but can be approached by emphasising different aspects to those currently overvalued. The reconsideration of the role that fashion and style plays in the subversion of socio-cultural values should lead us nearer to the authentic poetry of architecture.

One of two week-end houses at Garraf Barcelona by J.L. Sert and J. Torres 1935. Pioneer architecture for an 'ideal client' and a revolutionary society which resulted in a formal success but a verbal failure when that society was silenced from without.

Thirty years later.

A permanent revolutionary attitude is present in the novel diagonal form of the suspended staircase that stimulates the code of domestic architecture. *Casa Augusti*, 1955, Sitges, by Josep M. Sostres.

If architecture could be written it would not be built[1]. With this severe limitation in mind the author invites the reader to share this written architectural dialogue in the hope that we can meet half way along the way towards a critical understanding of the other side of architecture. To suggest that architecture, or rather the critique of architecture, has two sides is not to mean that they are opposing sides, rather that there are two complementary sides. On one hand there is the patron, the public, who has to live in it, shared with the non-architect professional critic, where he exists, who tries to explain it all (the verbal), and on the other hand there is the architect who is actually creating it (the formal). The author, as a practising architect, is on the latter side, the other side, and with this book risks trespassing on another's field, treading on a few toes, breaking the rules, and ignoring all the delights of speculative analogy, in fact, all that is proper to the present occupiers. But confident that this is a minor evil in the face of the general environment self-destruction with which it is apparently associated by some critics of society, the author affirms his faith in the progressively higher objects of architecture in providing a coherent cultural and poetic setting for its human actor.

Having emerged from the neolithic condition, the age which traced its course with fire as the principal source of energy, humanity began to live in a new humane and cosmological condition, helped by the second industrial revolution with its instant communications. According to Teilhard de Chardin's phraseology this can be called noosphere. We are more sensitive to good and to evil, and to progress and to regress, concerning the whole rather than concerning a part of humanity. On the negative side, who does not share the guilt of the brutality of the wars in Vietnam and the ex-colonies of Africa, and the racial rejection of the "foreign" immigrant?

Not for nothing are the peace movements and student unrest universal. Not for nothing are the peasant Pope John and the guerrilla doctor Che Guevara heroic figures throughout the world. We are more sensitive, but we must be much more so if we are to be sensitive to the positive as well as to the negative aspects of the noosphere.

The extension of this new mentalization forced by a permanent revolutionary attitude of the minority necessarily has its own casualties, the utopians and avoidists, and the pessimists. Architecture too has its utopians and avoidists and its pessimists. If these casualties are understood and, rather than rejected, are assimilated, the higher objectives and consequences of a profound and universal civilization will be all the richer. In the same way that it belongs to no one man to possess the whole truth so it is that each one has a part of it. That surely is the essence of real social democracy with its respect for the individual as an inter-dependent member of the community. It is this acute sense of inter-dependence that leads architects and their architecture into a desire for an effective role in society.

Casualties of the revolution—
architecture that avoids reality in
a formal make-believe world. *Casa
Cruylles* (18)* by Antoni Bonet—an
effective romantic escape.

A sick architecture that courts reality
with formal irony and a certain amount
of despair. *Casa Belda* (17) by Miguel
Alvarez—a visually satisfying drug
architecture of evasion.

The evasive pessimism of Marcuse's
ambiguous linguistic encounter with
the repressive tolerance of the consumer
society becomes a fading force clinging
to the utopian pleasure principle, itself
alienated from the "nonsense" of
reality. ("*Occidente*" 1967 by Solbes
and Valdés, private collection, Madrid)

*Bracketed numbers e.g. Casa
Cruylles (18) refer to the numbered
schemes beginning on page 24

It is sufficient to note here that architecture cannot be marginal to society. It is, along with everything else, an inherent part of it. Its tragedy, hence its pessimism, is the rejection of its total role by so many, including many so called architects, who reduce this mother of Art and civilization to a pathetic "woman of the streets". These professional prostitutes are the dismal half products of a lop-sided civilization where the sensitiveness of Teilhard's universal mentalization has not penetrated. The abrupt extension of environmental patronage from aristocracy to the masses after the post-industrial social revolution has not been accompanied by what Herbert Read calls "Education through Art"[2]. The subsequent loss of cultural values is obvious.

These half products, the half-architects, half critics and half-patrons shy away from reality with either arcadian or utopian, intolerant, linguistic affirmations which make written architecture so difficult to understand and built architecture so difficult to read. Perhaps these rather awkward terms, half-architects, half-critic and half-patron (or half public) should be further explained. The term half is used to imply the incomplete or uninformed limitation of each, whether acknowledged or not, who in order to personalise the multitude of ideas, or opinions, schematise them into simple forms that are easier to retain. There are those who acknowledge this limitation, and often cushion themselves against error by introducing a prudent uncertainty into their schemata, as against those who simply fail to realize this limitation. They run the danger of either opting out of culture altogether by not having any opinion at all or by adopting a dogmatic anti-dialectic attitude.

However, the role of the halves is not unimportant: on the contrary, besides throwing things into sharp relief with the stimulation on their controversial positions due to the simple structure of their interpretations, they invite the easy mental participation of the listener or reader, in contrast to the boredom inflicted by those who profess to be realists. After all, reality is often shown to be just facing up to what one thinks one knows about all along. The only hope for an active realist is to throw doubt upon the current concept of reality itself. In this way Alice's encounter with the Red Queen is not very different to Herbert Marcuse's encounter with the consumer Society[3], and one has to rush with both to be in the same place. Only Alice has an effective sense of optimistic humour that Herbert lacks[4].

This rushing to be in one place is the only constant in the inconstant reality, and is the secret of its dynamic interest as opposed to the static, even if sometimes valid, position of the extremists. As we shall see later, an extremist position is simply the over-emphasis of one of the parts of total reality. It is within this category that we find the exalted demagogic trends of National Romanticism, with its dead-ends in National Socialist and Peoples Democratic architecture, and the trends of Technological Romanticism with its dead-ends in a neutral architecture stillborn owing to the limited scope of "Information Theory" which, like Methodology, dwells only on existing data, and also Utopian Fantasy which never seems able to emerge from its pseudo-scientific test-tubes.

It may seem odd to accuse technology, which is seen to be the supreme manifestation of man's recent rapid progress, as being static. But it is nonetheless true, especially when technology is romantically offered as the twentieth century messianic solution to every problem. Dynamism is surely brought about between the changing relations between various parts, and however *progressive* technology is in itself it remains static and without interest in architecture as soon as it becomes the dominating element.

This dynamic quality of reality defies its own definition not because it is difficult to grasp because of its complexity, but because it is difficult to keep up with. We are born new every day and the existing context was yesterday. Architectural realism is therefore both dynamic and limited. Architectural realism deals with the existing context, or situations, as Norberg-Schulz[5] prefers to call them, which take into account the intrinsic values and relations between the economical, political and social conditions together with the cultural and physical conditions. Architectural realism has of course to define the building task and solve it with a formal structure but that is not enough to turn the building into architecture. The relationship between the two needs a further quality. It is this quality that Bruno Zevi describes as poetic. Zevi goes on to define architecture as the co-existence of poetic and non-poetic elements.[6] To deny the validity of the poetic content of architecture is to fail to understand the other side of architecture, the creative side. Here too realism can play a part. Poetic realism is that which dwells in existing situations charging them with imagination and suggesting the purpose of culture. Finally, realism must ensure that the communicative language of architecture should not be stretched beyond the range of comprehension. Sincerity of purpose is demonstrated when prolonged interest is maintained in a building, and then architecture becomes legible.

Although architecture cannot be written, it can be written about afterwards. Creative architecture is always one step ahead of the printed word, otherwise it would be banal. With this in mind and running along with Alice and the Red Queen we will try to keep up with the poetic (undefined ?) and non-poetic (defined ?) realities of architecture.

Since reality needs both the Alices and the Herberts, the author has chosen the unlikely subject of the living environment induced by recently designed private houses in Spain as a paradox, to explain the political and lyrical content of architects' architecture as opposed to the glossy consumer article. To do this, and at the same time avoiding the close-ended statements of the committed will be a difficult if not doubtful activity, but the reward for writing the obvious, and perhaps the not so obvious, will be worth it if it helps the reader to share in the active nature of architecture.

"Gestalt psychology" has taught us to be aware of reality as only one of the parts in individual work and its necessary inter-dependence on others within various systems, therefore underlining the inherent difficulty of defining reality itself. Also there is no clear-cut division between the real and the apparent consumer-needs nor between the dialects of social subversion and preservation, when material form has to be given to the "poetic idea". Architecture, too, is human in the widest and deepest sense, and can be neither more nor less objective, subjective, or neutral than its human source itself.

This essay on architectural criticism will not be based on any hard and fast principles, gentle and not so gentle manifestos. It is just an architect looking at his art for the 1970's. What emphasis it will have will leave aside professional competence, which is presumed to exist, to suggest a syntactic criticism that will be built up from an analysis of the semantic symbols of fashion together with those of social subversion as a step towards a clearer vision of the true poetry of architecture.

"It takes all the running you can do, to keep in the same place". Lewis Carroll's Red Queen understood the relativity of space and time to reality which is constantly evasive to those who think that by standing still they remain in the same place. (illustration from original edition by John Tenniel)

1. see the essay "Architecture without buildings" by Nathan Silver in the book *Meaning in Architecture* 1969 Barrie and Rockliff.

2. see HERBERT READ: *"Education through Art"*

3. see HERBERT MARCUSE: *"One Dimensional Man the Ideology of Industrial Society"* Sphere Books Ltd. edition 1968.

4. see the *American Anarchist manifesto* published in *Heatwave* no. 2 Oct. 1966: "HUMOUR" : the dynamite and guerrilla warfare of the mind, as effective in its own domain as material dynamite and guerrilla warfare in the streets".

5. see CHRISTIAN NORBERG-SCHULZ: *"Intentions in Architecture"* Allen & Unwin Ltd. (second printing 1966) p. 21

6. see BRUNO ZEVI: *"Architecture as Space, how to look at architecture"* Horizon Press N.Y. 1957 p. 221.

## 2. TOWARDS A DEFINITION OF THE DEFINED

SUMMARY
The definition of the fragmentation of mental attitudes in the verbal and formal context of architecture follows Bruno Zevi's analysis of political, philosophical-religious, scientific, economic-social, materialist, technical, physio-psychological, formalistic and spatial interpretations. The vocabulary of the more definable aspects of reality is reduced to its elements to enable a structural analysis and comparison of the built objects treated in this study to be undertaken.

One of the clearest definitions of the tangible aspects of architecture occurs in Bruno Zevi's simple masterpiece of critical writing *Architecture as Space*[1]. While recognizing that, for a fuller understanding of architecture, it is necessary to take into account the sum of many values with its ever changing emphasis, now here, now there, following the tides and currents of life, Zevi himself pleads the case for a super-interpretation of the concretization of these values through their relations in space. He further defines these spatial relations, together with their objectives, by testing them through the method of comparative history, from architecture without internal space (monument to Victor Emmanuel II Rome) to the organic space of modern architecture (Frank Lloyd Wright's "Falling Water"), in all, a spectrum of sixteen different defined objectives. To understand the reason behind these changing objectives (the poles of real and projected values) Zevi lists four premises—the social, the intellectual, the technical and the formal and aesthetic ideas—that should be submitted to critical analysis. After this, each individual work, he suggests, should be specifically evaluated according to its spatial relations with its environment, and within itself, together with an analysis of its enclosing volumes, decorative details and reference to human scale.

This critical super-interpretation of Zevi's is joined to, and compared with, eight other interpretations. These form an acceptable and wide enough base upon which a definition of the defined can be developed. Zevi lists six of them as interpretations of context, (1) Political (2) Philosophical-Religious (3) Scientific (4) Economic-Social (5) Materialistic (6) Technical, plus two more, (7) Psychological and (8) Formalistic. He then injects his own (9) Space as a super-interpretation of them all.

The author now proposes to narrow the context of this part of the introduction in order to relate this pluralistic basis of the defined to the specific context of the Spanish-built living environments illustrated in this book.

First we will consider the political context: Zevi defines the political interpretation as concerning the "cause of architectural currents or the symbolism of its styles". One only has to recall the German National Socialist persecution of the modern movement with its repression of the Bauhaus, or Mussolini's encouragement of a patriotic, stripped classicism that throttled the early Italian rationalism, to realise that the modern movement in architecture must contain a political interpretation to merit such attacks. Hitlers' blood and earth culture, Mussolini's Italic-Imperial anachronic revival, and Stalin's Socialist Naturalism, snuffed out the modern ("International") movement in favour of their local academic form of romantic nationalism. In this context it should be remembered that the kernel of the modern movement was its social-political conscience, as Le Corbusier wrote in 1923:

"Society is filled with a violent desire for something which it may obtain or may not. Everything lies in that: everything depends on the effort made and the attention paid to these alarming symptoms.

Architecture or Revolution
Revolution can be avoided".[2]

But the immediate answer to the threat of revolution was not architecture but repression.

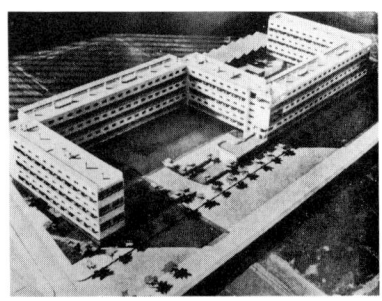

The new style architecture of the Republican government creatively contributed to the formation of a new style society. Workers' dwellings grouped around two spaces give the individual a physical sense of becoming a part that matters of the community. The *Casa Bloc*, 1932–36, Barcelona by architects of G.A.T.E.P.A.C.

Casa Villaró in Barcelona by Sixte Illescas, 1928, captured the essential elements of the rational styled architecture.

Air Ministry building Madrid, 1943—51, by Luis Gutiérrez. It was no coincidence that Paul Bonatz, the Third Reich traditional regionalist architect, intervened in the design.

Casa Ugalde, 1952, Caldetas, Barcelona, by J. A. Coderch and M. Valls. The surrealist formal effects were deliberately sought after in a desperate rejection of the social and cultural realities of the moment.

Symbols of the hollow grey élite of meritocracy are the affluent, faceless buildings that undermine the social morale of the modern movement. H.Q. of the Banco Atlántico, supposed symbol of "Opus Dei" in Barcelona.

In Spain the strong virile political impulse given by the Republican government from 1931—39, especially by the autonomous Catalan government, to a rational-social architecture through G.A.T.E.P.A.C.[3] (experimental housing and Casa-bloc, Tuberculosis Clinic, and in town planning, a Regional Plan for Catalonia, Plan Maciá for Barcelona by Le Corbusier, and a plan for Barcelona's parallel town for relaxation) was all brought to a sudden end by the uprising of the Generals on the 18th of July 1936. The bitter civil war was fought for ideals. Three years later some ideals were lost to be replaced by others. How is it that three decades later; in a country that till now retains an autocratic rule of law run on a confusion of orders, there is no longer an official rhetorical-monumental architecture like that which produced the Ministry of Air building, or "blood and earth" architecture like the Brunete housing in Madrid in the 'forties? After a decade of silent recovery and isolation, the rejuvenating spirit of the

Brunete Housing Madrid.

Valle de los Caidos. 1939—59. Monument to those who fell in the civil war with place of honour to José Antonio, founder of the Falange. A monument that explains too eloquently the mentality and pathos of an epoch.

rebuilding of Europe seeped through. The odd magazine, or visit abroad after the frontier was opened in 1948, kindled the flame for the visit to Barcelona in 1949 of Gio Ponti, Alberto Sartoris and Bruno Zevi. Consequently, a small group of architects gathered together to attempt the rebirth of the modern movement under the title of Group R[4]. The military and economic pact with the United States in 1953 paved the way for a new semi-economic and semi-cultural development, necessarily politically limited to the submissive bourgeois class. However this gave room for fringe intellectual, cultural, and even political, activity for a very small minority.

Casa Guardiola, 1955, Argentona, by Josep M. Martorell and Oriol Bohigas. The return of functional expressionism within the Mediterranean cubist language of the 'thirties.

Casa M.M.I. 1958, Barcelona, by Josep M. Sostres. A revaluation of De Stijl was one of many of the leaps backward to sources that the rebirth of modern architecture underwent to establish a vocabulary in post-isolationist Spain.

During these formative years Spanish architecture slowly relearnt the vocabulary of the modern movement. The third decade concerned itself with the meaning of this vocabulary. As the blood and earth dictatorship eased a way to admit the creeping electronic dictatorship of the Opus Dei[5] under the watchful eye of the Pentagon, and the American and European capitalist élite, the new affluence of an unequal society undermined the effective social role of the modern movement. The alienation of culture from society needed no Marcuse to uncover the reality of the situation. A political interpretation of current Spanish architecture would point out the symbols of a sporadic guerilla warfare in the use of a subversive language that sets out to break the established codes, for those that are interested. The lack of communication tends to make politics a rhetorical question; the result is pessimism. Reality rather than Utopia is clearer as a result.

Subversive language of urban guerrilla warfare sets out to break the established codes—anarchy assimilated. *Meridiana Flats*, 1963, by M.B.M.

Subversive language of suburban guerilla warfare sets out to break the established codes—shock tactics of reality—hipster jazz with face to the sun, backside to the street and a laugh at sick architecture. *Casa Penina* (22) L. Clotet and O. Tusquets.

Two Spains, neither Europe nor Africa, but the antithesis of conflict, together with the status quo of the centre, Castilla, and the turbulent cultural periphery, Andalucia, Portugal, Galicia, the Basque country, Aragon and Catalonia. Contrast the culmination of the Christian pilgrimage route—*Portico de la Gloria, Santiago* Cathedral 1188 with the *Giralda of Seville,* symbol of Islam 1184—1196.

The philosophical-religious interpretation concerns that part of architecture which is the visual aspect of history according to Zevi. This is broadly taken to mean that architecture responds to the immediate fundamental political changes as described above, at both the macro and micro levels of the culture to which it belongs. Architecture, however, also responds to history at another almost undefinable plane, the historical-geographical level. It is what Nikolaus Pevsner simply calls the geography of art,[6] and what Unamuno calls the eternal tradition[7] (the unity of the past-present and future) which lies in the "intrahistory" of man.

The elusiveness of this "intrahistory" is confirmed by the immediate contradictions that spring to mind from diametrically opposed historical examples. Undaunted and with Chestertonian relish, Pevsner demonstrates that it is only through accepting these paradoxical examples, or polarities as he calls them, and by studying and analysing them, that "one can in the end arrive at a complete definition of character". Thus he has been able to define the Englishness of English art. It is beyond the scope of this introduction to define convincingly the Spanishness of Spanish Architecture but it is possible to indicate its polarities and to arrive at an approximate definition.

The first thing to remember is the well known observation that there is not one Spain but two, the centre, and the periphery. The flat, broken Meseta 2.000 ft up is Castille: around it lies Andalucía, Portugal, Galicia the Basque country, Aragon and facing the Mediterranean civilization, Catalonia. The second thing to remember is that Spain separates Europe from Africa, rather than uniting them, because of the Pyreneés and the mountainous character of the interior with no natural E—W or N—S traffic routes. From the first group of polarities arise the internal peninsula conflicts between the unifying attempts of Castille and the cultural and economic independence of the periphery. From the second group of polarities of being neither in Africa nor in Europe and as a consequence having suffered a 500 year conflict with Islam, arises the lack of compromise between dogmatic attitudes. These geographical polarities mark the Iberian character and its architecture. From the first group we have the focal points of conflict between the artificial and isolated centre of Madrid and the pragmatic magnetic attraction of Barcelona. From the second group the eternal antithesis of African and European cultures, as seen for example in the Portico de la Gloria of Santiago Cathedral (built 1188) the culmination of the great Christian pilgrimage route and the Giralda de Sevilla one of highest symbols of Islam (built 1184—1196).

Bernard Bevan dismissed the question of Spanish originality since he considered that the "history of Spanish architecture consists in its major part the study of foreign influences and the history of its naturalization"[8]. This was anathema to Fernando Chueca who set out to prove the opposite in his unique study of Spanish architectural invariants[9]. He accuses Bevan of being obsessed by the incomplete character of Spanish history which failed to close any biological-evolutionary cultural cycle. Chueca simply points out, that cultural cycles (if admitted) are not necessarily confined to any geographical limit. A summary of Chueca's invariants of Spanish architecture would include the characteristic tendency to the compartmented space not only horizontally in plan but also vertical in section, with its resulting casual compositions accentuated by the use of the broken asymmetrical axis. The articulation of the spaces in between brings townscape into buildings making each one of them into city-like

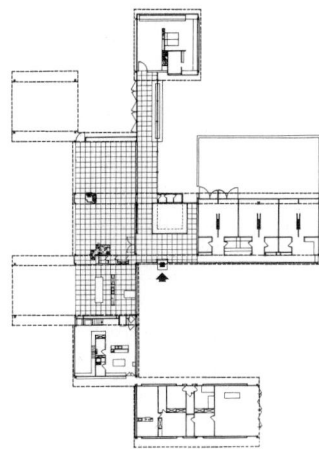

Spanish invariants—city-like houses or square, compartmented spaces on a broken asymmetrical axis. *Casa La Ricarda*, 1959, by Antoni Bonet.

*Saló del Tron.* The great 14th century reception hall in the Royal Palace, Barcelona. A civil architecture free from imposed connotations and open to a sense of economy gave a compact anti-rhetorical form to Catalan architecture.

*Casa Catasús,* 1958, Sitges, by J. A. Coderch and M. Valls. Economy of form, intimate and, like the *Saló del Tron,* anti-rhetorical, this house follows the disciplined tradition of Catalan architecture within the syntax of modern architecture.

*Casa Lujan*, 1961, by M.B.M. Architectural form reduced to the binary program system of day and night is too primitive a synthesis for the ambiguous cultural and social values of the user.

convents, city-like palaces and city-like farms. Chueca goes on to underline the sincerity of volumes, their cubic treatment, and the geometrical (Euclidean) discipline with the dominance of the right-angle and tendency to squareness (note the Spanish horizontal gothic). In the matter of decoration he points out two polarities, the tendency to concentrate in areas of contrast as against the tendency to run wild with atectonic confusion. Pevsner too has pointed out the two major polarities of Catalan architecture, on one side the exuberant modernism at the turn of the century (works of Gaudí, Doménech, Jujol) compared with the disciplined Gothic between 1240 and 1400 (works of Ferrer, Carbonell, Sagrera, and the earlier works of Fabre and the English Fonoyll).

Here it is interesting to quote from a young Spanish critic Lluis Domenech[10], writing on the constants of Catalan architecture, who seems to agree with Bevan but adds significantly a great deal more.

He refers to two historical reasons. "First, the constant problems of territorial integrity and political independence which leave no time for original creative culture, but give an agility in rapidly assimilating and synthesizing ideas produced in the rest of the world. Second, the preponderance of the civil over the religious or monarchical client which clears away imposed connotations, leaving the way open for a sense of economy in the process of design and construction. These two historical reasons, apart from others, have enormously conditioned the tradition of an architecture which has maintained the characteristics of being compact, intimate, anti-rhetorical, and ambiguous at the moment of choosing a primary global form, open to many meanings, and sifted through an innate sense of economy, internally conditioned by its own technological elements and use".

He further deduces that there exists a structural relationship between this local cultural phenomenon and the attitudes adopted towards this phenomenon during the design process that leads to the final concretization which he likes to call a "constructive logic". This structure, Domenech suggests, gives a characteristic dialectic effort to the act of designing, the result of which is conditioned in such a way that it is capable of defining architecture in its formal and stylistic aspect, without having to resort to abstract ideas or borrowing from the allied arts.

Although more words have been dedicated here to the historical geographical level of the philosophical-religious interpretation in order to probe the values of local springs in the current cultural streams of western civilization, this should not be interpreted as a bias. On the contrary the incisive visual and linguistic investigations taking place within other geographical limits are more often the more fertile sparking points of the dialectical process of creating a new architectural object. When the invariants of the "intrahistory" rise up to become a major part of instant history, architecture dies sterile, and we have another "blood and earth" junk house.

Gathered together ambiguously under the title of scientific positivism Zevi groups the interpretations based on the mathematical and geometrical basis of architecture, the economic and social basis of architecture, and the expansive materialist (geographic, geologic, building materials, functional, archaeological, racial, etc.) basis of architecture. Just as every interpretation is valid so long as it is not exclusive, so the mathematical approach has its limitations. The romantic adolescent fashion for a computer-based architecture with its comic strip visual companion has distorted its fundamental, serviceable role in the ordering of the functional content of architecture. Architectural problems may be reduced to the binary system for better analysis and a proposed synthesis of form but never in exchange for cultural synthesis by its human designer[11] The vast fields of mathematical inclusion embrace nearly every step in the creative process of architecture. Although it would be unacceptable to suggest that they all form part of the language of architecture, since many of its symbols have diametrically opposed meanings, it would be wrong from a realist view to deny the service value of its vocabulary. For example, and to use Charles Jencks' coinage, the New Palladians follow Rudolf Wittkower's use of the mathematical systems of proportion for their symbolic rather than their abstract value. The Academic Platonists reduce the fixed parameters to a minimum to create an indeterminate structure capable of coping with change". . good design is reducing complex problems to simple, independent variables through systematic analysis". This backed up with cybernetics, is extended as a new moral preconception for the academic method of arriving at a logical (?) built form. Another mathematical vocabulary which, if overstressed, is likely to be the agent of its own destruction, is the process of designing using the axonometric cut-away techniques of the popular illustrations of mechanical inventions. This method, as Jencks point out, "allows the architect to work out the space, structure, geometry, function and detail altogether and without distortion."[13] The danger is that, while it forces the imposition of the third dimension with its spatial volumetric consequences, it freezes the viewpoint, usually an unrealizable one from the sky, at the expense of the play of scale in the fourth dimension of movement through space.

"Architecture is the autobiography of economic systems and of social systems".

That "architecture is the autobiography of economic systems and of social systems"[14] is self-explanatory and needs no explanation if the role of architecture were limited to the passive production for uncritical consumption. But is all production and its consumption uncritical? *"C'est pour toi que tu fais la revolution"* writes Cohn-Bendit. "There is no such thing as an isolated revolutionary act. Acts that can transform society take place in association with others, and form part of a general movement that follows its own laws of growth"[15]. This collective, critical attitude springs from the anti-university which, having analysed their own problems, "the logic of their conclusions drives them on ultimately to reject the whole of contemporary society." This same pessimism is apparent in architecture, too, as James Stirling wrote in 1965, ". . . I think architecture at the moment is rather static because I think architects are cynical about the society which they have got"[16]. So it would be truer to change Zevi's phase to "architecture is both the autobiography of economic systems and of social systems *and its criticism*".

The material interpretation is found in the early functional, later international, organic and technological schools of architecture. The "Form follows Function" creed of Sullivan is well known but since it has incised so sharply into all modern architectural thinking it is worth quoting Carl Condit's interpretation of the Chicago architect's philosophy.

> "The proper understanding of the word *function* is the key to his whole philosophy. An organic architecture, he believed is one that grows naturally or organically out of the social and technical factors among which the architect lives and with which he must work. These factors embrace not only the technical and utlitarian problems of building but also the aspirations, values, ideals, and spiritual needs of human beings. Thus *functionalism* involved for him something wider and deeper than utilitarian and structural considerations, important as these are"[17]

In other words every building has its fitting, or typology, and so its form. The International style that developed three decades later arrived at similar conclusions but with certain parametric cultural values that conditioned the typology of all buildings.

For Frank Lloyd Wright, the scion of Sullivan, Organic Architecture meant in addition a harmonic composition with the site and a preference for natural materials and sympathetic environment for human sentiments. However Organic Architecture is better understood in its full historical sense through the examples of its main proponents, Wright himself and Alvar Aalto. It is in these works we can observe the meaning that "the inner nature of the problem always carries the solution itself".

The technological and mechanical interpretation, which glows in Ruskin's *Lamp of Truth,* on the other hand aims at expressing the maximum potential use of the instruments adopted, be it a new material like steel, reinforced concrete or plastic, or a new system of designing, or a new building method, or simply a complex communication structure.

This brings us to the end of the pluralistic contextual interpretations suggested by Bruno Zevi. These together with an intentional spatial interpretation are all part of the current vocabulary of the modern movement, and so apparent in one way or another, with more emphasis here, and less there, in the houses examined in this book.

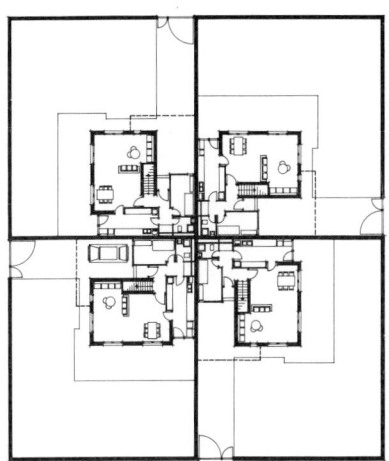

House group near Tudela by R. Moneo. Sociofugal plan that discourages the formation of human relationships for, in spite of its formal grouped composition, each looks out away from the neighbours.

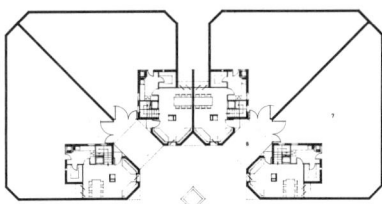

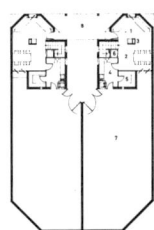

Rural house group at Gimenells near Lerida, by Sabater, Domenech and Puig. Sociopetal plan that encourages the development of human relationships by looking into a shared space with the neighbours.

Ever since doctors demanded green paint for their patients rooms, architects have looked askance at the psychological help offered by the medical profession. Zevi soundly dismisses it to the sphere of aesthetics away from the field of architectural criticism. But if we accept the dialectical auto-critical process of design, architectural psychology cannot be dismissed so lightly. Much of the vocabulary of the behavioural sciences (psychology, sociology and anthropology) is common to the designer's explanation of his work. The natural consequence of this is to include this growing vocabulary as part of the motive if not actually the object, of environmental design. The theory of empathy is fundamental in this respect in establishing the relation between the identification of the user of the object with the intentions of the designer of the object. As an example, the work of Izumi and Osmond in the field of architectural psychology and its therapeutic effect of environment on the mentally sick is important in defining with more precision the social intentions of architecture. Quoting from Kenneth Bayes' excellent study on the subject,[18]:

"They have divided building plans into two types,—sociofugal and sociopetal. Sociofugal plans discourage the formation of human relationships . . . (railway stations, airports, transit hotels etc.) . . . . . A sociopetal plan, on the other hand, is one which by its arrangement and shape of rooms encourages the development of stable human relationships. The prime example of this is the family house. Homes and schools for exceptional children and mental hospitals should also belong to this category. A sociopetal layout is not one which allows no privacy where people are thrown together all the time and cannot get away. The growth of interpersonal relationships depends in a community, on being able to slip away easily and unobtrusively from one to another of three separate zones of sociability—complete privacy, the intimate group, and the larger group".

Bayes goes on to discuss the principle of transition between the zones with particular reference to entrances. "The entrance to a building, the threshold where—whatever transition zones there may be in the form of courts on one side or foyers on the other—the out side and the inside meet is very significant. On a different level, it is akin to the other boundary crossing experiences of going to sleep, waking up, being born and dying. This feeling has led, in the architecture of the past, to the enrichment and emphasis of entrances until they have become the main feature of the façade. Within our own idiom, the entrance should still be positive and significant. Especially with maladjusted children, where occasions should be emphasized, rhythms felt, festivals celebrated, actions clarified and articulated, the design of the entrance should enhance the action of coming in and going out.[18a]

This same principle can also be applied, to a modified degree inside a building for maladjusted children, to the entrances to each living unit or group, if only by widening the corridor, a special door detail, or change in floor level, so that the children pause and notice . . . . ". Bayes also quotes Aldo van Eyck.

"To go in or out, to enter, leave or stay are painful alternatives. Though architecture cannot do away with this truth, it can counteract it by appeasing instead of aggravating its effects. It is human to tarry. Architecture should take more account of this".

These problems of community and privacy are developed in the book of that name by Serge Chermayeff and Christopher Alexander which bears the significant sub-title "Toward a New Architecture of Humanism".[19] The event (1963) indicated that the time in the story of the modern movement had come for a softening up of the frigid discipline of the early years.

To avoid the diffusion of different zones by blurring the transitional phase, Bayes goes on to consider the psychological reactions to ambiguity. (Osmond and Izumi sharpened their experiences by taking LSD.) where confusion of identification are disturbing or even frightening. Architectural character and scale naturally come within the compass of architectural psychology, as do room sizes and shapes and, above all, in the negative aspect, that terror of the endless corridor with its Kafka dream image of the destruction of time and space and ultimate death.

**Zevi's dissatisfaction with the naive concepts of the traditional formalist interpretations such as unity, symmetry balance, emphasis, contrast, proportion, scale, expression, truth, propriety, urbanity and style, is taken up at length by Norberg Schulz[20] who**

suggests the more sophisticated concepts of *Elements* ((1) more or less concentrated mass (2), more or less closed space (3) surface) together with their *topological relations* (proximity, closure, fusion, division, succession, continuity and similarity) and *geometrical relations* (organization of elements relative to a point (centralization) or to a line (axiality or guiding elements) or to a co-ordinate system (systematic use of parallel lines). The different combinations of *elements* and *relations* create an infinite number of *Formal Structures* (cluster, group, row, both closed and open) at different levels depending on the relations. The formal properties common to a collection or works form a *style* where elements and their combinations with a symbol-system appear with varying degrees of probability.

The object of this pluralistic resumé of the definable has been to establish a minimum agreed vocabulary upon which we can proceed to investigate the values of the undefined, and an inspection of current trends in architecture, so that a proper evaluation of the following Spanish examples can be made.

1.   BRUNO ZEVI: *"Architecture as space, how to look at Architecture,"* Horizon Press, NY, 1957.
2.   LE CORBUSIER: *"Towards a new Architecture"* Architectural Press. 1946 edition. p. 268, 269.
3.   G.A.T.E.P.A.C.—Grupo de Arquitectos y Técnicos Españoles para el Progreso de la Arquitectura Contemporánea, founded in 1930, see Carlos Flores' *Arquitectura Española Contemporanea.* Aguilar p. 135 and ff. see also ORIOL BOHIGAS: *"Arquitectura Española de la Segunda Republica"* Tusquets Ed. 1970
4.   Group R—see ANTONI DE MORAGES I GALLISSA "Els deu anys del Grup R d' Arquitectura. Serra d'Or Nov/Dec 1961 p.66.
5.   OPUS DEI: An association (founded by *José María Escrivá* which significantly became effective in 1939 with the revised publication of *Camino*) that promotes the individual religiosity of its members and the conversion of others from the seats of power, which it believes is the most effective and efficient method. As a consequence, the acquisition of power is justified as a means to an end. Evangelical, theological and sociological considerations make the theory and practice of "Opus Dei" historically morally and ethically doubtful.
6.   NIKOLAUS PEVSNER: *"The Englishness of English Art"* Ed. Peregrine Books 1964 p. 15 and ff.
7.   quoted from FERNANDO CHUECA: *"Invariantes Castizos de la Arquitectura Española".* Dossat. Madrid 1947.
8.   Idem.
9.   idem.
10.  see LLUIS DOMENECH: *"Architecttura civile e logica construttiva"* L'Architecttura, Jan., 1970, Rome.
11.  CHRISTOPHER ALEXANDER with his early warning missive *"The Synthesis of Form"* that startled not a few into a godworship of the computer as the messianic savour of architecture, an unintentional result that Alexander himself sought to correct in his essay "A much asked Question about Computers and Design" published in *Architecture and the Computer,* Boston Architectural Center p. 52.
12.  CHARLES JENCKS: Pop-Non pop. *Architectural Association quarterly* Winter 68/69 p. 54 and ff.
13.  idem p. 62
14.  BRUNO ZEVI *Architecture as Space.* p. 167
15.  GABRIEL and DANIEL COHN-BENDIT: *Obsolete Communism. The Left Wing Alternative.* Penguin Books, 1969, p. 249.
16.  JAMES STIRLING: *R.I.B.A. Journal,* May 1965. p. 238.
17.  CARL CONDIT: *The Chicago School of Architecture.* University of Chicago Press, 1964, p. 37.
18.  KENNETH BAYES: *The Therapeutic Effect of Environment on Emotionally Disturbed and Mentally Subnormal Children.* Design Research Unit 1967 p. 13.
18a. IVAN NELLIST: *"The Planning of Buildings for Handicapped Children".* Crosby Lockwood, 1970.
19.  SERGE CHERMAYEFF and CHRISTOPHER ALEXANDER: *Community and Privacy.* Pelican Orignial, 1966.
20.  NORBERG-SCHULZ: *Intentions in Architecture.* Allen & Unwin, 1967.

## 3. TOWARDS A DEFINITION OF THE UNDEFINED

SUMMARY

We cannot grasp reality without leaving it open to an element of unreality, that constant leap into the free space of imagination. By probing the harmonic preconscious life of the intellect the institution of real, rather than alien, poetic intuition can be made available to everyone. Architecture too is open to real poetic intuition and it is in those buildings, that contain it that the soul of architecture can be discerned.

*Casa Rozes* (2), by J. A. Coderch and M. Valls. The poetry of place.

"If architecture was born of need, it soon showed some magic quality, and all true building touches depths of feeling and opens the gates of wonder".[1] The style dates Lethaby's phrase, except that the indication of there being something more to architecture than service, points to the identification of the originality of man with the originality of his work.[1a] A man is a man is a man, not less, perhaps more. Originality is not rational. So we are all mad, its just a question of degree.[1b] If the sane wait for Godot, they may, like Sartre's Pablo Ibbieta, devalue life by rejecting magic and wonder which are discarded as deliberate attempts at self-deception. It is rejected because the work is seen to have been given an energy beyond its capacity which makes it "an instrument of an alien spirit. . . .a sacrament of a separate poetry which makes a game of art,"[2] — and, if one may add to Maritain's words, a game of life. Without identification it is opium for the lesser man.

This alienation of man from the proper realm of his imagination is, in the words of Marcuse, "the obscene merger of aesthetics and reality (which) refutes the philosophies which oppose 'poetic' imagination to scientific and empirical Reason".[3] Just as the irrational becomes the home of the rational, so reality lies in the unreal, and for man, the man, the optimist and adventurer poetry is the light of ultimate freedom.[4]

Following Maritain's steps let us consider two thoughts on poetry. Shelley in *A Defence of Poetry* wrote:

*Casa Vilaseca* (11) by M.B.M. To create anew through the renovation of tradition. The open-enclosure of the Renaissance balustrade is approached with the use of moulded pre-cast concrete balustres hung from steel railings inverting the structural logic of the original while retaining the spatial ambiguity between solid and void.

"Poetry defeats the curse which binds us to be subjected to accident of surrounding impressions. And whether it spreads its own figured curtain, or withdraws life's dark veil from before the scene of things, it equally creates for us a being within our being . . . It creates anew the universe, after it has been annihilated in our minds by the recurrence of impressions blunted by reiteration".[5]

And Emerson in *The Poet:*

"The poet has a new thought: he has a whole new experience to unfold: he will tell us how it was with him, and all men will be the richer in his fortune. For the experience of each new age requires a new confession. and the world seems always waiting for its poet. . . .

"We are symbols and inhabit symbols; workmen, work and tools, words and things, birth and death, all are emblems; but we sympathize with the symbols, and being infatuated with the economical use of things, we do not know that they are thoughts. The poet, by ulterior intellectual perception, gives them a power which makes their old use forgotten, and puts eyes and a tongue into every dumb and inanimate object . . . As the eyes of Lyncaeus were said to see through the earth, so the poet turns the world to glass and shows us all things in their right series and procession. For through that better perception, he stands one step nearer to things, and sees the flowing or metamorphosis . . . "[6]

By poetry, we mean, along with Maritain, "not the particular art which consists in writing verses, but a process both more general and more primary: that intercommunication between the inner being of things and the inner being of the human self which is a kind of divination . . . the secret life of each and all the arts; another name for what Plato called *mousike.*"[7]

Arcadian applied poetry, an alien
style from without, shows itself in the
playful experiment of form and detail
independent of Norberg-Schulz's
institution. *Casa Garreta*, 1969,
Altafulla, Tarragona, by M. Alvarez.

In moving along towards a definition of this process, Maritain claims that "the intellect, as well as the imagination, is at the core of poetry". He adds "but reason, or the intellect, is not merely logical reason . . ."[8] which takes us into the depths of the unconscious, not the automatic, animal conscious of Freud, but the musical, preconscious life of the intellectual. If this intellect intuition of Maritain is accepted, then the poetical intuition which leads on to the creation of architecture, is open to definition through a conscious intellectual effort. If we include the "Gestalt principle" concerning the structural interdependence of the parts to form the whole, especially in perception, and accept it, then a proper valuation of Norberg Schulz's effort to provide a structural analysis for an operative conceptual scheme is possible without the prejudice that we are killing creative intuition at the onset.

Following the classical procedure of structural analysis Norberg-Schulz defines the constituent units of the institution.[9] The primary model is built up from (1) the dimensions of the building task, (2) formal structures and (3) the relation between the two. Innate poetry, or real poetry, is created within this structure. Alien poetry from without, is either a very rare casual event, or is suspect—opium, as we have written before, for the lesser man.

The exhaustive creative process of a continual dialectic between analysis and decision (both in thought and on paper, during the long months of designing a building) is the battleground where the poetry of architecture is born. There is no easy way, and the final order out of chaos leaves few perfect objects.

Utopian applied poetry, an alien
style from without, shows itself in
the playful experiment of form
independent of Norberg-Schulz's
institution. Form for form's sake,
Sert's studio for Miró in Majorca,
1955. Developed with further
misfortune by the same architect
for the Maeght Foundation, Saint-
Paul-de-Vence, France 1959—64
and by Antoni Bonet for his
*Casa Cruylles* (18).

1.  W. R. LETHABY: *Architecture, an introduction to the history and theory of the art of building.* Home University Library. Thornton Butterworth, 1911 2 ed. 1934 p. 13.
1a. see JAMES STIRLING *R.I.B.A. Journal.* May 1965 p. 239: "It is more like a love affair with the building. Undoubtedly one is emotionally involved with one's building. I know this is so because when they are finished and the clients are about to move in I have a sort of resistance. I think they are going to do all the wrong things when they get inside. I keep coming back and hanging around, and probably pester the daylights out of them. Eventually it fades on you, usually you are getting involved with the next one, and after a period of time, maybe a year or so, I seldom go back."
1b. see R. D. LAING: *The Present Stress* quoted in *The Bomb Culture* by Jeff Nuttall, p. 110. Paladin Ed. 1970.
2.  JACQUES MARITAIN: *Creative Intuition in Art and Poetry,* Ed. The Harvill Press, 1954 p. 401. where J.M. quotes his earlier work *"La Clef des Chants"* in *Frontieres de la Poesie* (Paris, Rouart, 1935)
3.  HERBERT MARCUSE: *One Dimensional Man.* Sphere Books p. 195
4.  COLIN WILSON: *Introduction to the New Existentialism* Hutchinson, 1966 p. 176 and ff.
5.  JACQUES MARITAIN: *Creative Intention in Art and Poetry.* Collins, p. 146.
6.  idem p. 147
7.  idem. p. 3
8.  idem. p. 4
9.  see Norberg-Schulz: Intentions in Architecture.

## 4. SOUL ARCHITECTURE

SUMMARY
Style is the coherent language of fashion and its symbol system provides the key to the probable current relations between the different elements of reality. It is only when a style is confused as an element in its own right, rather than the vehicle that relates the elements to each other and that carries their interpretations to a proper understanding of the intention, that style becomes the corrupting force that devalues architecture.

Now we suggest that there is room for further investigation into the relationship between the creative arts, with special reference to architecture, and their efforts to express the common human paradox of personality plus conformity in the dynamic context of the moment. As part of this investigation it is here that we wish to revalue the concepts and attitudes to fashion and style, probe apparent superficiality in order to demonstrate its vital contribution to soul architecture—that architecture which breathes a poetic content.

Trend in search of a folk tradition that began with Tennessee Ernie's *Sixteen Ton* cowboy lyric and led on to Allen Ginberg's *Beat Generation.* Architecture squares up to the trend with Higueras' *Casa Lucio* (6).

When, in 1683, Claude Perrault, within the context of the Humanist debate over proportions, denied that "certain ratios were *a priori* beautiful, and that proportions which follow 'the rules of architecture' were agreeable for no other reason than that we are used to them, and consequently advocated the relativity of our aesthetic judgement . ."[1] he was just writing that we like what is fashionable. Good (interesting) architecture is that which is in fashion, bad (uninteresting) architecture is not, unless it is old enough to be historic: this attribute is often considered more important than whether it is good or bad. Discounting the mere "trendies", this apparently supercilious overstatement is right up to a point. It depends on the discreet distance that is kept from the point which determines the strong from the weak, and the weak from the very bad.

All architecture is free-wheeling and is in the full swing of fashion, and if not always setting it, at least it presents mature examples of it. However, few architects would care to go along with a Christopher-Alexander-like analysis and admit that they were self-conscious about it beforehand. Since *Haute Couture* is a tricky business, it is safer to make it an unselfconscious part of culture in contrast to the selfconscious working out of functional planning and rational structure. Hitchcock and Johnson burnt their fingers when they seriously called attention to the facts of life with their baptism of the vanguardist work of the twenties by naming it the "International Style".[2] It immediately became a term of abuse, so much so that even now Hitchcock prefers the use of "modern" for fear of being misunderstood. But now as we enter the seventies, it is ridiculous to sweep the term under the bed. Moreover, it is suggested, that style, the formal probability structure of a symbols-system according to Norberg-Schulz, is the coherent language of fashion, despite the inherent element of "designed uncertainty" (Meyer).

Free-wheeling with fashion may not be as exhilarating as the pace-makers but shows an awareness of where the life of culture is—be it underground—as against the anti-life of the establishment. The timber-shuttered column of the outsized porch of *Casa Carner* (10) by M. Ribas is an 'affront' to 'good taste'.

Even in the early days of modern architecture when all had to be destroyed for a bright new flapper world (except curiously Rome and the Acropolis), there was to be found amongst these pioneers of contestation the genius of Le Corbusier which filtered through his passion a recognition of the validity of a style in architecture. In the twenties there could only be one style, and one alone for the Bright Young Things and to establish it, he lashed out against the others with: "Architecture has nothing to do with the various 'styles'. The styles of Louis XIV, XV, XVI, or Gothic, are to architecture what a feather is on a woman's head; it is sometimes pretty, though not always, and never anything more". These phrases are repeated three times in the same book together with three reminders to architects on mass, surface, and the plan.[3] What he was attacking here was not style in itself but the anti-realists who lightly applied revival styles to a hungry consumer demand without culture. He pleaded for style, rather than non-style architecture. "Our own epoch is determining, day by day, its own style".[4] Only we do not see it", he complains. His verbal style, in the days of *l'Esprit Nouveau*, was the hygienic house as a machine for living in. "Demand a bathroom looking south, one of the largest rooms in the house . . . " begins his manual of the dwelling.[5] The ship, the aeroplane and the automobile are the fashion generators. Then for good measure and to prove that the new style was legitimate, Rome and the Acropolis were brought in as respectable godparents. The result was flat roofs, white walls horizontal ribbon windows, cut-back attics, double-height living rooms, and order through the desire for standard and modulated elements.

Another apology for the new style, though he refused to admit the word, was the Bauhaus hard-liner, Walter Gropius, whose defence of the flat roof now makes delightful reading:

> [1] "light, normally shaped top-floor rooms instead of pokey attics, darkened by dormers and sloping ceilings, with their almost unusable corners; [2] the avoidance of timber rafters, so often the cause of fires; [3] the possibility of turning the top of the house to practical account as a sun loggia, open-air gymnasium, or children's playground; [4] simpler structural provision for subsequent additions, whether as extra storeys or new wings; [5] elimination of unnecessary surfaces presented to the action of wind and weather, and therefore less need for repairs; [6] suppression of hanging gutters, external rainpipes etc., that often erode rapidly."[6]

Is it possible that Gropius really thought that these "practical" and "functional" reasons rather than fashion led him and Adolf Meyer to design buildings with flat roofs? The only valid point of the six is the possibility of using the flat roof for some open-air activity. If the roof is not to be accessible then economics dictate a pitched roof as the quickest and safest means of shedding the rainwater, as a good insulation, and finally as often the most economic structural form. The only occasion that would economically justify a flat roof is an irregular plan shape demanding the use of valley gutters, (the weakest point in any pitched roof design). No, Gropius was as fashionable in his architecture as he was with his clothes.

If we return to the beginning of the century, we find that we have run through a series of fashions both concurrent and consequent, which were a formal response to the inadequate cultural position of architecture. It must be remembered that an architects' architecture can only be fulfilled when either a unified or pluralist society agrees on a minimum dialectical base, the absence of which creates an uneven situation where struggle is the predominant link between this architecture and the society it is trying to change. Since this situation is the more frequent there is always something utopian or vanguardist about architects' architecture, however realist it sets out to be.

A characteristic of a successful vanguardist position is that it becomes a pace setter, or, in more usual terms, fashionable. This is turn becomes rapidly devalued, as the form rather than the content is understood by its followers.

A too detailed account of the various fashions from around the turn of the century to the present day would lead to a plagiarism of another's territory and would be beyond the scope and the purpose of this essay.[7] However, since the roots of the present non-mod fashion lie in this immediate past, it is necessary to run briefly through this history to keep up with the present, like Alice.

It is natural to begin with the French Revolution in 1789 with its immediate revaluation of the city and the ideal of citizenship. Current ideas determined fashion, and democracy was in the air with inspiration from the Greek city states and Republican Rome. Later, came Napoleon's expedition to Egypt which introduced a new oriental exoticism, and John Nash built the Brighton Pavilion for the Prince Regent. The circle of reaction after the revolution was completed with a new historical romanticism given impetus by Schiller's *Maria Stuart.*

The growing wealth and crudity of the bourgeoisie, based on the profits of the industrial revolution that could develop its own economy, now that the feudal barriers had been swept aside by the Revolution of '89, alienated the intellectuals. With Lord Byron as their hero, they cultivated a romantic melancholy, grew beards and long hair and adored the fragility of women, epitomised by the ballet *Les Sylphides* danced by Taglioni in 1827. Culture and fashion was split between the scientific positivism that grew from mechanical inventions, scientific discoveries, and Darwin's theory of evolution on the one hand, and on the other, the romantic religious revival that led on to the subversive Aesthetic movement.

Can architecture be free of fashion, be it action or reaction? The Bauhaus flat roof is the symbol of its rational technology that is now usually associated with the Establishment of modern architecture. The *Casa Ballbé* (7) by Tous and Fargas recalls the heroic period and is either a late example or early revival of that style.

Back to ornament with the functionalism of the particular with an expressionism that titillates with a devaluation of architecture. Detail from the *Casa Romeu* (4), by Milá and Correa.

The two cultures also mixed incongruously at times, as at the Oxford Museum. The battle of the styles that resulted from this split culture, turned some architects to take refuge in the virginity of engineering with its purity of materials. Ornament was the arch-enemy. Adolf Loos wrote his famous *Ornament and Crime* in 1908, which Le Corbusier picked up in his *"L'Esprit Nouveau"* in 1920. This contained the most powerful negative acid ever to be thrown upon architecture. Even now, half a century later, the word "ornament" is considered an anathema that would amount to nothing less than treason to the modern movement. Ornament cannot be burnt out of architecture, only now it has to masquerade under many a different label: texture, detailing, silhouette, pattern, colour

Other architects joined forces with the softer humanists, in despair of the evils of the exploiting industrial revolution and tired of inventions from the railway to the crinoline, they swung back to the primitivism and pure living habits of old mother nature. The Aesthetic movement, revolving around Rosetti and William Morris, and brilliantly exploited by Oscar Wilde, paved the way through Burne-Jones for the introduction to Paris of *Art Nouveau.* But this sophistication of the Naturalist School, abetted by Zola, was too fragile to endure the fascination for the new mechanics. After the Prince de Sagan rode his bicycle down the Bois de Boulogne amongst the horses the new aesthetic "functionalism" was in. The complementary sports of roller and ice skating and open-air tennis gave a young hygienic air to it all. Hermann Muthesius was sent over to England from Germany and found the quiet simplicity of the freer English domestic architecture cultivated by Philip Webb, C. F. A. Voysey and Norman Shaw.

Architecture was finding its "functionist" tradition. With the discovery of the Kimberley diamond mines wealthy merchants and financiers took over from the last of the aristocrats as pace setters, and eyes turned to the millionaires of the American Utopia. And from America came Frank Lloyd Wright, half expelled from the States in 1909, who unexpectedly appeared as the incarnation of the marriage between the new engineering and naturalism. This biological mix-up he called organic architecture, which sent a real flutter through young hearts, and still does, and will no doubt do so for a long time yet. Gropius and Meyer were among the first to set the trend going in Europe with their administrative building at the Werkbund Exhibition in 1914 with its wide brimmed roofs floating over strip windows and clay brick walls attempting to contain the building back to its earthly origins.

Another way to hug the earth was to let the walls wander out beyond the actual building, a favourite device of Wright, which was copied notably by Mies van der Rohe, even if somewhat more frigidly than the "Prairie" style architects would have approved of.

Other fashion setters opted out as visionary individualists to introduce an elementary mannerist expressionism. Their chunky streamlined buildings drew many in to dabble for a while.

Meanwhile around the perimeter of the central European whirlpool a traditional non-plot plot was set between the co-edifying forces of Romantic Classicism and National Romanticism, in both the Scandinavian and Mediterranean cultures, with their by-products of Social Realism in the former and Fascism in the latter.

By the end of the twenties through the semantics of fashions, the syntax of a style was first perceived, and although its symbols have now mellowed, criticism of style in the seventies must begin here.

1. RUDOLF WITKOWER: *Architectural Principles in the age of humanism.* Tiranti, 1962 p.144
1a. see JAMES STIRLING: *R.I.B.A. Journal.* May 1965 p. 240 ".... I never select materials emotionally; they are chosen *entirely* at a practical level, . . . ." (the italics are mine D.M.)
2. HENRY RUSSELL HITCHCOCK and PHILIP JOHNSON: *The International Style,* Ed. W. W. Norton & Co. N.Y. 1966, which includes the essay "The International Style Twenty years After" by H. R. Hitchcock reprinted from *Architectural Record,* August 1951.
3. LE CORBUSIER: *Towards a New Architecture.* Architectural Press (1946 edition) p.p. 27, 37, 45.
4. idem. p. 9 and p. 89
5. idem. p. 114
6. WALTER GROPIUS: *The New Architecture and the Bauhaus.* Faber and Faber 1935, p.29.
7. JAMES LAVER: *Taste and Fashion.* Harrap, 1945.

## 5. THE FIRST "INTERNATIONAL STYLE", ITS ELASTICITY AND EVOLUTION

SUMMARY

By leaping into the free space of imagination and inventing a prototype vehicle that communicated the revolution of the elements of architecture, the pioneers of the twenties did an immeasurable service to the art and science of architecture. The reality of style was rediscovered. Its enrichment is called for rather than its rejection.

The attempt to prove the obsolescence of history-orientated values within the context of vanguardist architecture is as unconvincing as the substitution of pigeon-English instead of English as a basis for a literary work. The latter-day scientific positive attitudes of Buckminster Fuller, the Archigram group, and the fringe work of Reyner Banham are too restricted to form a basis relevant to a free creative architecture. That is not to deny the value of their imaginative contribution to the whole; what would be misleading would be to deduce that it is the whole. Fuller's and Banham's criticism of the International Style (of the 'twenties) because it failed to take account of the full potential of technology, is a little empty beside their own unviable, and politically regressive approach to the future. If we accept that there is something more in architecture than geodesic structure, Machine Age Plumbing, Environment-Bubbles and Cushicles, then a look at the values that the "International Style" provided, can be fruitful.

Although the parents of the International Style, Oud, Le Corbusier, Gropius and Mies van der Rohe have died, and although its historians, Henry-Russell Hitchcock and Philip Johnson, now admit that the International Style is over, its theoretical assumptions and practical achievements have been so incisive in the modern movement, that no serious criticism can ignore its presence within all consequent architectural design. The designer can choose to accept part of it, or can rebel against all of it, but in either case it is there and still asking awkward questions about the formal responses to modernity.

Hitchcock and Johnson in their book on "the International Style" point to three formal characteristics: (1) architecture as volume as opposed to mass, (2) regularity as opposed to symmetry and (3) the concern for the intrinsic elegance of materials as opposed to applied decoration. Few would argue with these values but most have something to add forty years later. Writing only twenty years later Hitchcock suggested that he would now prefer to omit the reference to ornament and substitute it for articulation of structure.

A few quotations from this lively book of the period provides stimulating reflections— it was art alive to fashion. Influenced by skeleton construction and the possibility of screen walls we find that:

"The prime architectural symbol is no longer the dense brick but the open box".

"The clarity of the impression of volume is diminished by any sort of complication. Volume is felt as immaterial and weightless, a geometrically bounded space. Subsidiary projecting parts of a building are likely to appear solid. Hence a compact and unified solution of a complex problem will be best aesthetically as well as economically".
*Vulcanized rubber corsets for tubular dresses and architecture*
".... as a corollary of the principle of surface of volumen there is the further requirement that the surfaces shall be unbroken in effect, like a skin tightly stretched over the supporting skeleton".

Order was to be achieved through relative regularity rather than axial symmetry;
". . . technically the prime architectural problem of distribution is to adjust the irregular and unequal demands of function to regular construction and the use of standardized parts.
". . . aesthetically expressed in a visible regularity and consistency. This is the symbol of the underlying technics, which in the completed building are known rather than seen".
*Shingle hair, trousers and two seater sports cars for functional girls and architecture.*

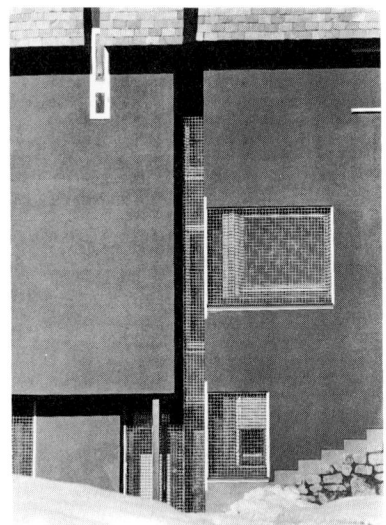

Skin surface with stretched laced 'see-through stockings' over the windows is going towards a sensory aesthetic in architecture. Detail from the *Casa Heredero* (19), by M.B.M.

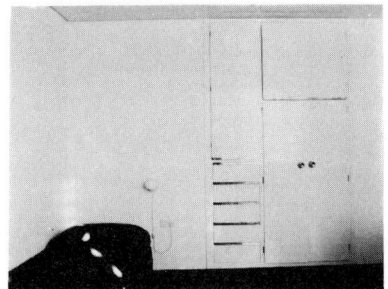

The elimination of ornament follows Loos after neo-liberty into his world of erotic art. Loos mistook the clothes for the crime, but his naked architecture was more erotic than anything he attacked. The light touch and decoration of the interior of *Casa Bricall* (21) by C. Cirici is provocative.

What is beautiful was ugly before—the roof projections of *Casa Dahl* (13) by J. Bonet follows Charlie Parker in debauching the dogmatic prescriptions of Art with the free lyric of improvisation.

*Casa Orpi,* 1962, Figaró, by M.B.M. An echo of the chunky, raw buildings and naked services of the New Brutalists— an apparent revolt against the International Style with form, material and detail.

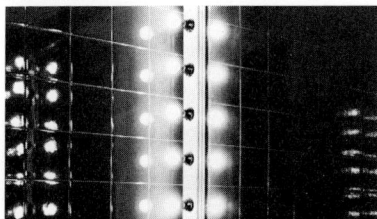

Pop or Gestapo-style brain-washer? The same destructive environment for sub-culture as for square culture? Naked light of the 'twenties (Banham) Las Vegas (Venturi) or just theatrical fun from Philip Johnsons's bathroom? Anyway here it is again in *Casa Penina* (22) by Clotet and Tusquets.

It was in the relativity of the principle of regularity that Hitchcock and Johnson foresaw the elasticity of the discipline of the style.

On decoration, where Hitchcock now has second thoughts, the authors wrote:

"decoration may be considered to include not only applied ornament but all the incidental features of design which gave interest and variety to the whole. Architectural detail, which is required as much by modern structure as by the structure of the past, provides the decoration of contemporary structure".

*Silk stockings, short skirts for the erotic-aesthetic of young leg and architecture*

"Those who employ roof projections in normal construction indicate a definite lack of feeling for contemporary style", unless it is extended as a plane as in the Barcelona Pavilion.

*Russian boots and German brims were awkward exceptions*

"Kirche, Kinder Küche!" the reaction swept in. Where has our long-haired mini-skirted architecture got to? Has it gone sick or underground?

From construction to destruction and then from the ashes to reconstruction, a shattered modern movement adapted itself to the economic realities of quantity and dabbled in a romantic national rationalism based on what J. M. Richards called "the logical next step, the functionalism of the particular" and adapting the whole to the existing environmental context. In Rome, Zevi back from exile in the U.S., founded the Association for Organic Architecture, and the architectural values of Frank Lloyd Wright and the Scandinavian countries were fashionably sown on the fertile soil of a tempered international style. Meanwhile Mies van der Rohe and Philip Johnson with their respective Farnsworth and New Canaan houses brought the ordered monumentalism of the International style to an apparently final solution.

The evolution of the International style seemed impossible, and even Philip Johnson who named it, wrote "Long live change" in 1961. The collapse of C.I.A.M. at Dubrovnik in 1956 over disagreement on the Athens charter introduced a more deterministic approach. It was almost as though the International style had to be attacked in order to bear the new generation. The New Brutalists literally attacked the "sacred" prisms of the twenties and thirties with their chunky raw buildings and their naked services. Le Corbusier himself with his Maison Jaoul and the Ronchamp chapel seemed to flout the so called principles of the International style. Through abuse and immitation the International style became a dirty word. But has this attack been valid? Is it possible to separate the modern movement from the International style? The style of the modern movement is surely both beyond the national and within the history of its beginnings. Although it is rooted to the local socio-cultural context, its dialectical investigation evolves in a higher stratum common internationally through almost instant communication.

This may of course be a play on words, and even if it is then nothing is lost, as it is suggested that the intention rather than the emphasis is really the same. The fault lies in the attempt to write architecture clearly instead of ambiguously building it. It began with the Johnson and Hitchcock book, but traces of it can be found everywhere, not least in the present article. However one example will suffice to illustrate this point of confusion.

Reyner Banham, whose lively historical criticism enriches so much of the current written architecture, has recently written about one aspect of the International Style:

"In the end, pure white light was to survive only as the weapon of the Secret Police interrogator, the brain-washer, and the terrorist. But before that regulation to the underworld of Western culture, it had almost a two-decade career in the visible and progressive overworld, as architects of the International Style—with the noblest aspirations, and clear consciences which the clarity of the light was supposed to symbolise, no doubt—subjected doctors, art-collectors, publishers, teachers and the other law-abiding bourgeois who were their clients, to a Gestapo-style luminous environment, with light streaming from bare, or occasionally opalescent, bulbs and tubes, and glaring back from white walls. Even when allowance is made for the specialised purposes of exhibitions, which may have needed unusual intensities of lighting, the published record of the work done by the Bauhaus and like-thinkers down to 1934, combined with the memories of survivors, leaves an impression of a luminous environment close to the threshold of pain, probably made tolerable only by the notorious willingness of intellectuals to suffer in the cause of art".[1]

However colour and indirect lighting were often used in many of the buildings of the twenties and thirties—Sert's buildings in Barcelona in the thirties, to cite just one example.

Also the published record of one of the Bauhaus thinkers reads differently to Banham's description. Lazlo Moholy-Nagy wrote in 1925:

"Colour in architecture helps to create a sense of comfort to suit the room and its occupant. It thus becomes a coequal means of spatial composition which can be further supplemented by furniture and materials. The origin of contemporary experiments in painting the walls of rooms in different colours is as follows:

"The effect of rooms painted homogeneously is hard. There is too much self-emphasis in their uniform colour, In such a room the presence of the single colour, whatever it may be, is constantly with us. When however, the various walls are painted in various harmonizing colours it is only the *relationships* of the colours which operate. A resonance arises which displaces colour as a self-accentuated material and creates instead an effect in which colour relationships alone play a part. This gives the whole room a sublimated, atmospheric quality: comfortable, festive, diverting, concentrating, etc. Some system in the choice and distribution of colour is determined by the room and its function (hygiene, lighting, technique, communication, etc.) It follows that the habit of painting walls in different colours cannot be indulged everywhere indiscriminately".[2]

The first internationals set out to strip architecture of its overloaded bourgeois historical connotations and attempted to communicate with the broader necessities of contemporary society, forging its way towards a new and better world. They faced the reality of the situation and heroically scratched together a primitive architectural vocabulary as a new medium of communication. This aesthetic vocabulary was at times as crude and often as primitive as was necessary for the great leap forward into living history. Turning the sprint into a marathon is a process of enrichment rather than of rejection.

It is suggested that the social and aesthetic aims of the International style for the alternative society are still valid because they are capable of evolving beyond the first ideas of the pioneers and although tempered by local political and fashionable cultural realities, have survived to continue progressing on a universal front. The name is now no longer necessary, it has passed into history, but the movement it started remains a dynamic style throughout the world. Its values are to be found in what is common to its opposite poles of expression.

1. REYNER BANHAM: *The Architecture of the Well-tempered Environment.* The Architectural Press, 1969 p. 129.
2. LASZLO MOHOLY-NAGY: *Painting Photography Film.* Lund Humphries, 1969. first note on p. 18.

# 6. CONTRADICTIONS IN LIVING ENVIRONMENT

SUMMARY

The paradox of the combined aspirations for asserting individuality as a personal contribution to the progress of the community and identification through conformity with the collective aspirations of the community itself forms the basic contradiction in living environment. The situation is complicated when the personal assertion is of doubtful efficiency and when the collective aspirations of the community are dispersed or non existent. Those objects that face up to and absorb the reality of the contradictions fulfil the function of built architectural criticism in setting the environment in a new order.

"The house is an institution, not just a structure, created for a complex set of purposes. Because building a house is a cultural phenomenon, its form and organization are greatly influenced by the cultural milieu to which it belongs. Very early in recorded time the house became more than a shelter for primitive man, and almost from the beginning "function" was much more than a physical or utilitarian concept. Religious ceremonial has almost always preceded and accompanied its foundation, erection, and occupation. If provision of shelter is the passive function of the house, then its positive purpose is the creation of an environment best suited to the way of life of a people—in other words, a social unit of space".[1]

In writing this, Amos Rapoport has paved the way for a revaluation of the house as worthy of architectural study beyond a mere instrument of anthropological research. Although he splits buildings into those of the grand design tradition (the culture of the elite) and those of the folk tradition (culture of the masses) and concentrates almost exclusively on the latter to show "the link between form and life patterns", the former should not be necessarily excluded. Just as behaviour and form are linked on a reversable relationship by either first understanding the behaviour patterns to understand built form (form follows function, Sullivan), or, by observing how form affects behaviour and a way of life (function follows form, Mies), in the same way there is obviously a reversable relationship between the subculture of the elite and the subculture of the masses. In both subcultures men sleep, eat, work, love, pray, wash, dress, talk and move as social beings responding to and creating their own interrelated living environments. The aspirations of both subcultures are probably very much the same if we discount the conservative struggle of the powerful to retain their distance from the masses. The worker has little interest in conserving the division of labour and expresses his own paradoxical contradictory aspirations of individuality and conformity in echoing the tastes of his leaders. One example of this can be found in the English workers refusal to wear a boiler-suit on the way to work, and sometimes even for work, unlike his continental equivalent, as a poetic and profoundly human protest against his loss of status in the anonymity of the first (dirty) industrial revolution. The laboratory assistant's white overall on the other hand symbolises his gain of status in his acceptance of the second (clean) industrial revolution.

These contradictions and ambiguous solutions that spring from the consciousness of belonging to one or other class, or subculture, are found in what Rapoport calls the primary forces that give the resulting form" . . . . . house form is not simply the result of physical forces or any single casual factor, but is the consequence of a whole range of socio-cultural factors seen in their broadest terms". "This form" he adds is in turn modified by secondary or modifying forces like climatic conditions (the physical environment which makes some things impossible and encourages others) and by methods of construction, materials available, and technology (the tools for achieving the desired environment).[2]

On the other hand the identification through form with the community has become increasingly difficult as the world eased out of its neolithic condition at the turn of the century and the collapse of traditional form itself began. The greater number of building types too complex for tradition opened the way for really new typological

The transfer of symbols from one subculture to another constantly revalues their significance and makes fashion move. Here, sophistication is given to 'rustic' materials and forms. *Casa Santorja* (8) by Higueras and Miró.

Ambiguity between assertive individuality and identification with the community (avoiding scandal) is happily achieved. A new prototype for Great West Road suburban architecture? *Urquia and Garcia houses* (20) by Sabater, Domenech and Puig.

images (hospitals, schools, offices, airports, factories, etc.), and the loosening of a traditionally shared undeclared value system (open restrictions) encouraged a demand for a non-traditional declared (closed restrictions) planning and building control system. Influenced by the concurrent new architectural typology, provoked to overcome the monotony of an unimaginative planning code, and spurred on by a new urgent sense of lineal, progressive, and above all evolutionary, time concept, society introduced a socio-cultural premium on originality. Instead of venerating his ancestors man pays homage to his future. The heroic optimism that needs to accompany the dispersion of the unleashed energies required to cover the probabilities of an uncertain future brings in its wake its own insecurity. Security is best found in a present alive to the past. We thus have to live ambiguously in the present, between the two poles of attraction, future and past. Our new built environment cannot but help express this ambiguity.

As a result of the uncertainty of the aims of the individual and the community in designing a house, or rather a home, the architect is faced with the most irritating, anarchic, ungroupable, crowd of problems. In no other building has he to design such a personal fitting for another human being. He is inclined to consider that the tailor-made home is an anachronism in the context of an age of mass necessity. While part of humanity, that which is exploited by the other part, lives either homeless or in apalling conditions of overcrowding, how can the architect who is culturally the best equipped member of society to solve these problems, spend six months or more of his time on a sort of anti-client who wants his own individual and original home? Instead of solving a straightforward problem of the simple necessities of sleeping and washing and cooking and eating with an additional space for looking at the T.V. and parking the car, the architect has to enter into the intimate dialogue that another human has with the world. This is an uncomfortable challenge to his own dialogue, but at times it is the only way to keep abreast with reality.

The whole structure of established social norms involving the individual and his complex relationship with others is brought into question in having to define the ordinary, physical details of life. Naturally not all the attitudes are in a state of flux and need new definitions, but even when the house itself is not considered a symbol of a "reactionary family structure" at least many of the established domestic practices are. The insecurity of the times has touched nearly everyone somewhere and this is reflected in both the definition and non-definition of private domestic domain.

### ATTITUDES ABOUT THE BODY
The body dressed and undressed, in private or in public (where do you undress to wash, community washing for the children, for parents: do you meet the guest in pyjamas in the passage?)
What is the bidet used for? W.C. and bath for reading?
Where do you put the clean and dirty clothes before going to bed? And shoes?
Does everyone really wash before eating?

### ATTITUDES ABOUT EATING AND ITS SOCIAL SYMBOLISM
Is breakfast a lineal event in the kitchen, a non-event, or a formal, tribal gathering?
If lunch or supper is the main family meal do the infants splutter in the kitchen and the elder children drift in later with a friend?
What about the social agony of eating with, or separate from, the home help who is no longer treated as a servant?
Where does a drink party or sandwich supper take place? On the stairs?
Is the proper place for the fridge the kitchen or the living room?
Food for survival or survival for food with tinned food, or French cuisine?

### ATTITUDES TO CLIMATE AND NOISE
For health reasons or fashion, is the sun to be welcomed in or kept out? Skin as white as a princess or tan with cream?
What degrees of ventilation and heating are required? Scents or smells and imitation coal fires.
How much noise can be tolerated? Fear of Silence.

### LIGHT
How much and what type of lighting and views are required?

The tailor-made home is an anachronism in the context of mass necessity unless the cultural challenge is met. *La Ricarda* (1959) by Antoni Bonet.

The whole structure of established social norms involving the individual and his complex relationship with others is brought into question on having to physically define the ordinary details of life. *Casa Ballvé,* 1957, Camprodón, by Coderch and Valls.

## LOVE AND SEX

What are views about sex, double beds? For those who say nothing, provide for twin beds, separate rooms for those who make a point of it, or even an enclosed bedroom garden court for those who want to venture outside.

Where should the child's bedroom be? Next to parents who will hear it crying, or well away, not to hear the tapes when it grows up?

## FAMILY TOLERANCE

How separate is the grandmother or single aunt, either living in or visiting?
Where do the children study separately?
Where do you practice the flute, have a children's party, read a book, sew a button?
Where do you go after a row?
Where does grandmother, aunt, husband, wife, son, daughter, entertain a personal visitor?

## FAMILY RELATIONSHIPS

What are views about status of women, distinction between man's and woman's domains (equality of sex is attempted if wife works and husband cooks: each has their own defined territory, den, and kitchen.)
What are attitudes to privacy within and without the house (freedom of action limited by responsibility towards others, the sharing of space and division of time).

## RELATIONSHIPS BETWEEN OCCUPIERS & SOCIETY

What are the territorial limits of entry at the garden gate, lodge, front door, no door?
How to provide for bells, telephone, TV, postman, milkman, meter-reader?
Are they extrovert and neighbourly or the opposite?
Is entry to the home encouraged or discouraged?
To fit in, or stand out
"Size" blown down or "size" blow up

Whatever it is, form must be given, defined in time and place.

Then since the home is to be situated in a place, the territorial attitudes towards that place have to be discovered and defined. It is unlikely that the architect and client have the same attitudes to everything, but since it is also unlikely that the client has fully realised his attitudes to life, in fact he is nearly always in a state of embroilic adventure, so a dialogue is usually possible when it is remembered that people usually decide to build a house between the ages of 35-45. To design a home for another calls for a dialogue beyond function and form into the realm of attitudes and values of life itself which are usually in a state of change. The ambiguous answers imply the necessity of a subtly arranged infra-structure upon which the variable relations can play and develop. From the uncomfortable test ground of a love-hate dialectic between client, together with grandmother, aunt, sister-in-law and son, etc., and the architect, can grow the most real of real architecture. It takes courage, as it took Frederick Robie to ask Frank Lloyd Wright to build "one of those damn Wright houses".[3]

Here lies the challenge for the architect. In other buildings he tests his ability to master technology, methods, community relations and specialization as well as the defined and undefined general values of architecture, but it is in the design of the private home that the formal consequences of the socio-cultural values are put to a supreme test. This explains why the successful encounter between different clients and the same architect leads to different formal results. Since there is no third party user, the design is the fruit of real participation of both architect and client. This participation is not proportional to the actual intervention of the client but it is proportional to the confidence between the two and the cultural level obtained.

In a world in need of shelters the creation of an unique architectural object as a personal home for one family is a grave responsibility for both architect and client. If the result is not a work of art, or does not at least have a certain didactic value, then society may indeed question the ethics involved. If the work is successful then it acts as a barometer of the present ethos and fulfils the function of criticism as T.S. Eliot understood it, in setting architects and architecture in a new order, readjusted to the current demands on the appreciated values inherent in the object. One building alone seldom fulfills this to become a master-object; they can be counted on the fingers of one hand, like the choir for the abbey church of St. Denis (1140—1150) just outside Paris where the Gothic style was finally "invented", and the nave of San Lorenzo (1421-60) Florence by Brunelleschi, where the Renaissance style was declared. Now in the seventies, is it a building by Sullivan, Wright, Gropius, Mies or Le Corbusier, or is it not truer and more appropriate to think of the plurality of the master-object more proper to the new age of man? But plurality does not liquefy the master-object to let it spill out into every object, as we are reminded by T. S. Eliot's rejoinder that "the majority of critics can be expected only to parrot the opinions of the last master of criticism; among more independent minds a period of destruction, of preposterous over-estimation, out of successive fashions takes place, until a new authority comes to introduce some order".[4]

Although writing about literary criticism, T.S. Eliot's observations are so poignant to the essence of the contradictory problem of the formal structure and language involved in the creating the physical and spiritual environments that we wish to live in, that it is worth quoting him further.

> ".... no generation is interested in Art in quite the same way as any other; each generation, like each individual, brings to the contemplation of art its own categories of appreciation, makes its own demands upon art, and has its own uses for art. 'Pure' artistic appreciation is to my thinking only an ideal, when not merely a figment, and must be, so long as the appreciation of art is an affair of limited and transient human beings existing in space and time. Both artist and audience are limited. There is for each time, for each artist, a kind of alloy required to make the metal workable into art; and each generation prefers its own alloy to any other. Hence each new master of criticism performs a useful service merely by the fact that his errors are of a different kind from the last; and the longer the sequence of critics we have, the greater amount of correction is possible".[5]

None of the selected houses pretends to be a diluted masterpiece, but they do all participate in going somewhat further than the usual consumer-article in showing that they are aware of the problems of architecture and its relation to the living environment ethos of the time and place. By comparison and analysis they each and all have something to say.

In a world in need of shelter the creation of a unique architectural object as a personal home for one family is a grave responsibility for both architect and client. Society may indeed question the ethics involved. *Casa Gomez* (1), by Saenz de Oiza.

1. AMOS RAPOPORT. *House Form and Culture.* Prentice Hall, 1969. p. 46
2. idem. p. 47
3. LEONARD K. EATON: *Two Chicago Architects and their Clients* M.I.T. Press, 1969, p. 11 for the actual quotation, but the whole book is a pioneer work on the "active" participation of the client in the creation of an architectural object.
4. T. S. ELIOT: *Selected Prose* edited by John Haywood. Penguin Books, 1953 text taken from: *The Use of Poetry and the Use of Criticism* (1933) under the title of *The Function of Criticism* p. 17.
5. idem. pp. 17, 18.

# 1 CASA GOMEZ Durana, Vitoria [Gazteiz], Province of Alava
1960
ARCHITECT: Javier Saenz de Oiza
CLIENT: Doctor, wife and three children

## SITE
3.000 m² (3587 yd²) barren semi-rural site some 7km (4.5 metres) N of Vitoria on the road to Vergada. The climate is windy and cold.

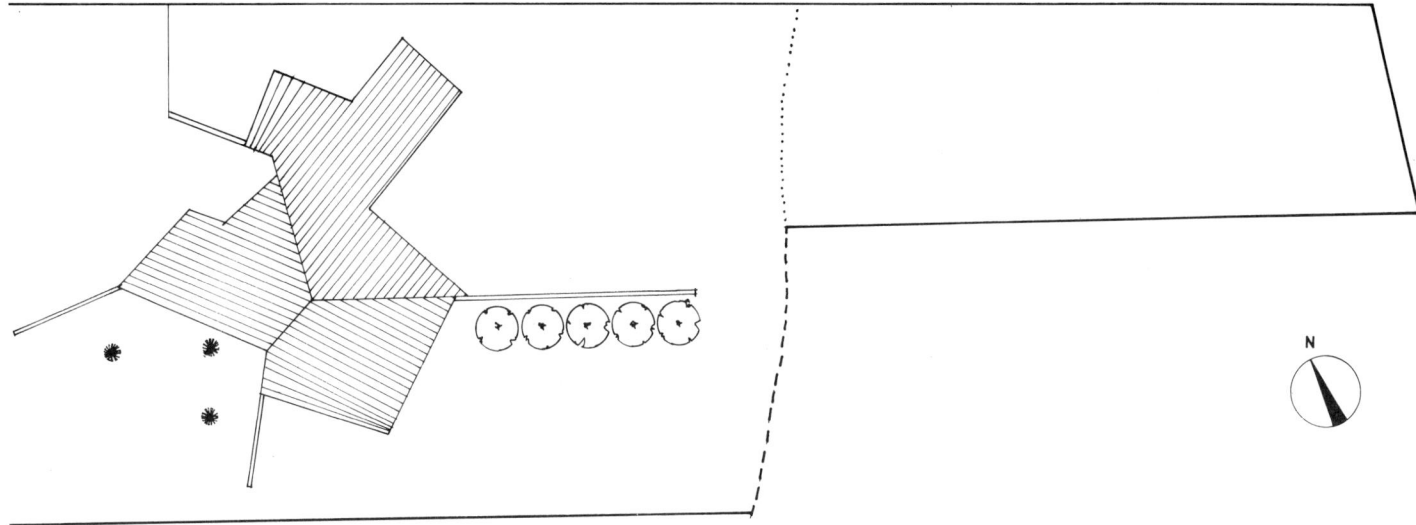

1.1    Site Scale 1: 500 and (facing)
       plan Scale 1: 200

## PLAN
In the words of the architect: "A concentrated plan that turns around the central chimney with structural walls spread out in the form of a spider's web with two or three concrete columns all of great simplicity that support a triple pitched roof. The enclosing walls are continued out to form three external spaces that correspond to the entrance and service (in reality two separate areas), the bedrooms, and the living area".

## CONSTRUCTION
Hollow brick load-bearing walls, with two or three concrete columns, covered externally with used pale yellow tiles and internally with pinewood sheathing.

## OBSERVATIONS
One might almost speak of the architecture radiating from Madrid as having an eclectic tradition from Juan de Villanueva onwards. The reason may lie in its splendid strategic isolation in the centre of Spain. With no grassroots it is not surprising that its architecture tends towards waves of experimental and cosmopolitian buildings that range from the brilliant to the barren. The latest wave started with the military and economic pact with the United States in 1953 that opened a fresh period of irrigation of Nordic (as opposed to Mediterranean) ideas of which the *Casa Gomez* is a typical example within this eclectic tradition. The dynamic spatial arrangement of the plan reflects Saenz de Oiza's admiration of Frank Lloyd Wright's organic approach to design, and the timber and brick detailing captures the strong post-war Scandanavian influence that was general in Europe at that time.

The centre of gravity around the fireplace is the basis of nearly all Frank Lloyd Wright's plans (derived in turn from the basic American home around the Franklin stove as typified by Catherine Beecher in 1869), but the extended spider-web walls owe more to the "de Stijl" compositional game with Lissitsky's object in space. It is as though Saenz de Oiza took Mies van der Rohe's similarly inspired brick house plan, shook it about and capped it with a pitched roof. All this, combined with an almost Scandinavian air, makes this undrawable building a real perplexing modern hybrid. The imperfect detailing of some of its parts is probably due to having to design "on the job". However, the unity of material, the dominating sweep of the roof, and the occasional sensitive touch just hold this restless building together.

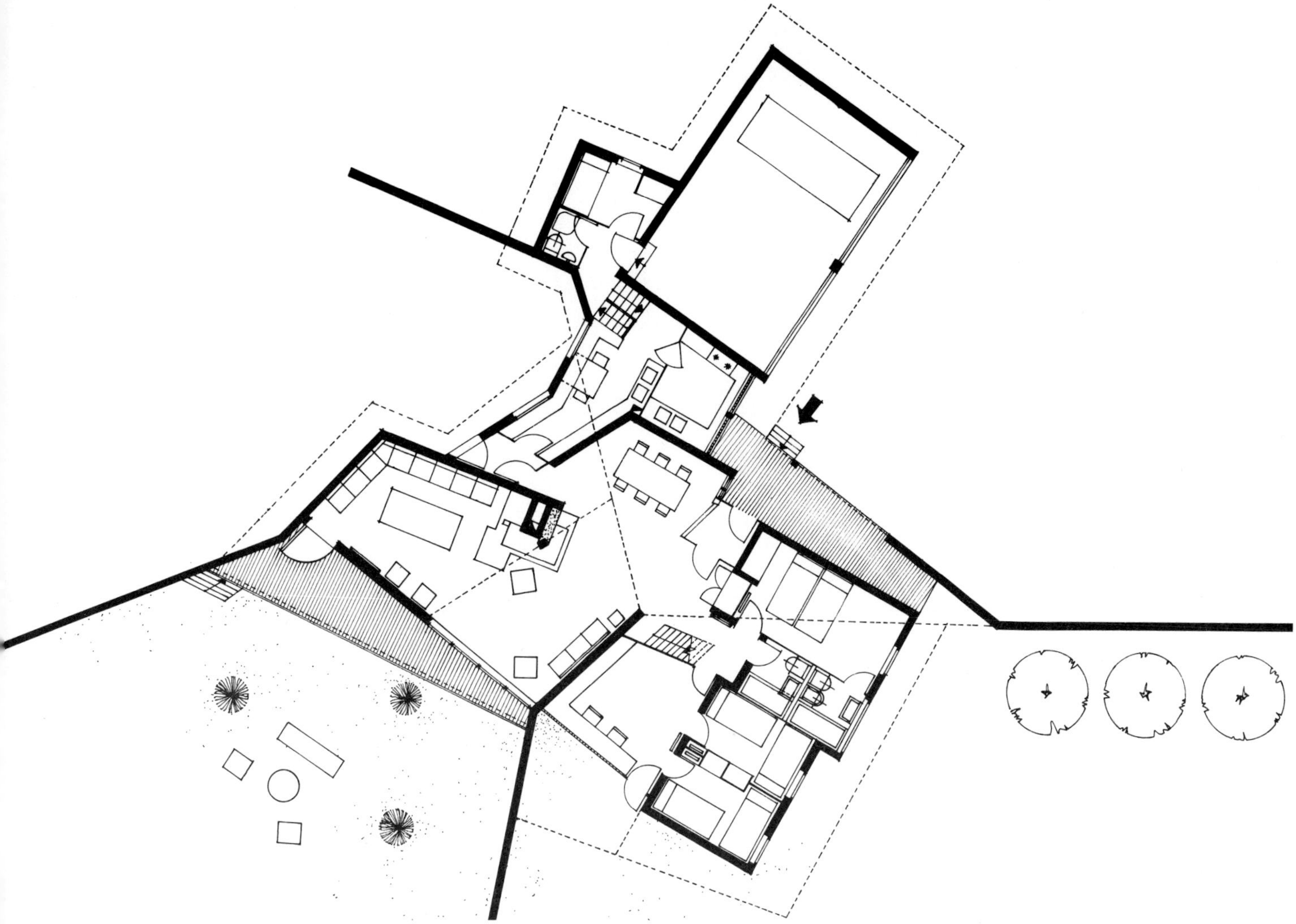

1.2 The entrance court from the East. The arbitrary position of the house in relation to the walled site limits is due to the overriding considerations of solar orientation. The garage doors are sliced off rather unhappily and the steps up to the entrance platform are rather odd.

1.3 The entrance porch. The scale, proportion, and simple detailing, are sympathetically handled apart from the steps. At the beginning of the 'sixties architecture, radiating from Madrid, tended to be somewhat eclectic with a noticeable lack of concern for place, but useful experiments were made, of which this house may be considered to be an example.

1.4 The living room court. The window to the upper right is a later addition to the original design. Inconsistent detailing can be noted in the abrupt ending of the brick dwarf wall underneath the terrace platform.

1.5 The central fireplace from which the living area radiates. An interesting play of space is obtained by separating the two focal points, the chimney and the apex of the roof.

1.6 The entrance area and lobby leading into the bedrooms.

## 2  CASA ROZES  Punta Canell Gros. Rosas. Province of Gerona
### 1961
ARCHITECTS:  José Antonio Coderch and M. Valls
CLIENT:  Doctor with small family (children 16 and 12 yrs. old)

### SITE
1.500 m² (1745 yd²) occupies three quarters of an irregular, rocky wave-swept promontory that completes one of the many small bays to the N of the fishing port of Rosas. The coastal protection laws, which define the limits of building encroachment, left only an elongated triangular area for the design of the building.

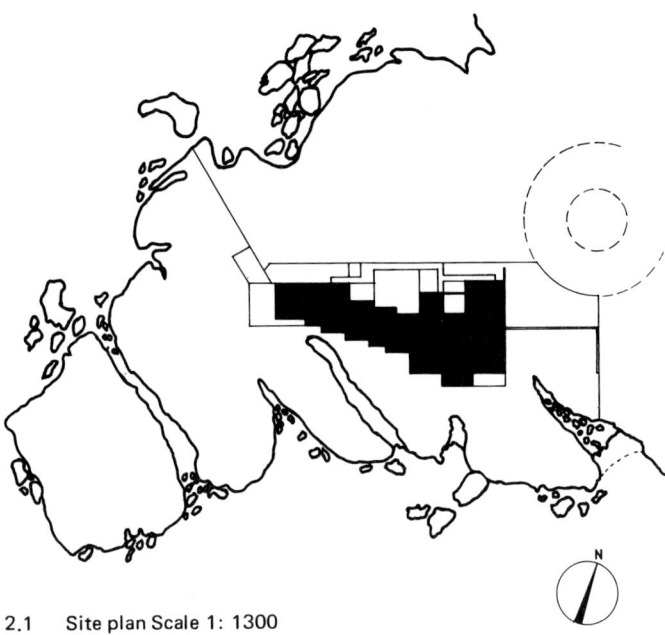

2.1    Site plan Scale 1: 1300

### PLAN
A linear plan that leads from the entrance and living areas down to the point of the promontory in a series of staggered steps incorporating a string of self-contained bedrooms, and terminating with the owner's suite with a boat-house below it.

As with nearly all Coderch's houses the entrance and garage coincide. Below the garage, facing SE, away from the hot afternoon sun, and with splendid views across an inaccessible precipitous coastline, the living area loops and drops around an internal planted court that filters the sunlight into this area. A service axis cuts across the house at this point with its entrance from the NW through the laundry area and enclosed patio to the servants' rooms and kitchen on the other side of the main corridor.

A series of guest bedrooms follow down the spine of an almost endless corridor which, at the same time, shields the rooms from the direct heat of the afternoon sun. At the apex of the house, there is a miniature living-sleeping unit as the owners' retreat.

### CONSTRUCTION
Cavity load-bearing walls, flat roofs with asphalt and pebble finish.

### OBSERVATIONS
The combination of blasted nature and architecture aloof from it, creates the overriding impression of awe usually reserved for monuments. Is it a home or an escapist's tomb

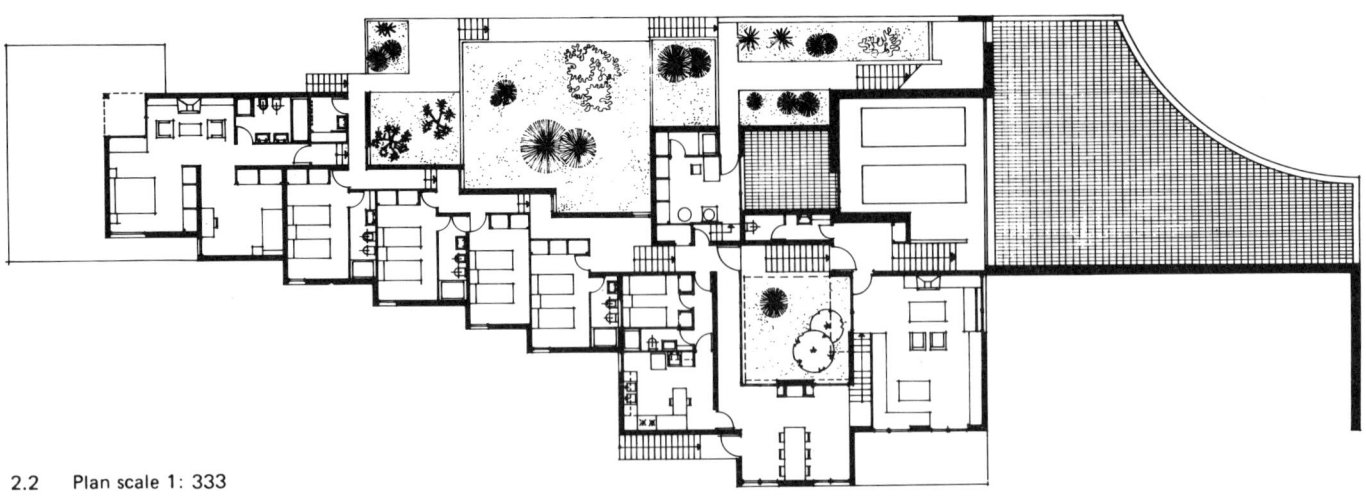

2.2    Plan scale 1: 333

that turns its back on its vulgar neighbours as a lonely protest against man's brutality to his environment? This admittedly subjective impression would be empty of meaning if it did not lead us on to appreciate the reality of the building's symbolism and its subversive challenge to those that opt out of culture at one level, and on a higher level of criticism, to those that hold too close to Wright's or Aalto's organic architectural creations.

Bred from the clean crisp naval influence of the first International Style, and the lazy volumetric casualness of the Mediterranean vernacular architecture, Coderch's built object has achieved a monumental sculptural grace as it triumphantly rides the crude majesty of its site. Its major symbol lies in its discourse with the natural environment. It takes two different people discussing the same subject to create favourable conditions for a fruitful dialogue. If one is only an echo of the other the conversation is a formal bore after the first exchange of information. This is one of the basic differences in attitudes towards the natural surroundings that lies between say, Frank Lloyd Wright and Le Corbusier. The former tends towards a monologue and the latter towards a dialogue. There are occasions for both, but here a mutual tension is set up between the site and the created object without, however, striking a discord. It is here that poetic intuition creates a corner of the universe anew.

2.3 The house from the East. To the right of the screen wall is the main garage—entrance and tradesmen's door, and to the left is the lounge with the interior court and dining area beyond and below.
The style of the house recaptures part of the fashionable vocabulary of the 'twenties which was popularised in the 'thirties. The influence of De Stijl is unmistakable, in the screen wall that partly destroys the isolation of the object in space, and the harmony of the cubes, surfaces and lines of the built-object itself.

2.4    The SE façade with the living areas in the foreground and the bedrooms descending to the left.
The cubic discipline and integrity of the formal structure is maintained even to the extent of eliminating the balcony railing and—that typical detail of the International Style—by ignoring the weathering of the coping. A note of constructive realism is introduced by cutting short the asphalt and pebble waterproofing of the roof over the balcony.

2.5    The house as seen from the end of the promontory showing clearly the string of bedroom compartments attached like a tail to the main body containing the living areas.
The addition of a casual cluster of compartments without loss to the object pole of the formal structure, of not wavering from the intentions of the modern movement, shows how a disciplined incorporation of some of the values of vernacular architecture can be achieved.

2.6    The main garage-entrance and forecourt. The surrealist effect of the ambiguous relation between form and function is effectively captured by the photographer. Traces of the same influences that moved Gaudí, Miró, Dalí and the recent *Dau al set* (seven-sided dice) movement are often to be found in recent Catalan architecture. Political and social exasperation often leads to the rejection of reality.

2.7 The NW façade, overlooking the bay, is protected by a series of garden boxes which are an integrated part of the sculptural whole.

# 3 CASA TAPIES c. Zaragoza. Barcelona

1961

ARCHITECTS: José Antonio Coderch and M. Valls
CLIENT: The painter Antonio Tapies, his wife and 3 children, eldest 7 years old (2 boys 1 girl)

SITE
250 m² (300 yd²) with 8m (26ft) frontage to a narrow street between party walls. The interior façade is SW the best for midday and afternoon sun.

PLAN
The space for the various activities, painting, social, and family life, is located on distinct levels. The ground level for which the building regulations allow a complete occupation, is largely taken up with the studio and its ancillary space for storage and packing. Under the house, which is shallower to conform with the regulations, is the entrance-garage and porter's lodge.

3.1    Section Scale 1: 200

The home, with the day space and bedrooms on separate levels, is on the first and second floors. The main living room extends out over the terrace that forms the roof of the lower part of the studio and is enclosed to form an outside room with a louvered ceiling. This terrace connects with a gallery in the high studio. The central staircase divides the service area with its laundry, kitchen, and servants' bedrooms, from the living and reception area.

Poised above the house, with an open play terrace for the children inbetween, is a second, reserved, living compartment containing a high library with a sitting area and a small secluded top-lit study.

The various levels are connected by a series of narrow single-flight deck stairs above one another and a lift. There is also a small service hoist.

CONSTRUCTION
Steel frame structure with the party walls infilled with exposed brick to the interior space.

OBSERVATIONS
Apart from the agile handling of the relationship between the studio and home, and the spectacular decision to float the library retreat above the house, the main critical attention should be paid to that old architectural problem of "facadism"

or the pastiche of façade architecture, that has been uncompromisingly used here by Coderch. The actual elements used are unmistakenly his own, but the idea of applying a screen to the building is a frequent urban solution to preserve the theatrical effect of the street as a stage for the community. The idea would be repugnant to purists of the early days of the modern movement, but now should be recognised as a genuine acknowledgement of the architectural role as a social agent to the urban scene.

The paradox of this house lies in the instrument of an artificial façade that is not used to communicate with the harmony of the street through using a similar vocabulary which, in this case, has little architectural merit, but acknowledges the urban scale through its minute attention to details, proportions, and artificial height of the screen, to avoid an unpleasant cut in the street wall: it is, in effect, a cage to keep the street out of the house.

This same spirit of introversion is present throughout the whole house with its wall and sky screens enclosing not only house but terrace as well. Is this a logical solution to the realities of climate and urban social environment, or is it an escape for one who can afford to withdraw into the impregnable privacy that approaches Michael Frayn's cosy sterilised nirvana of the Electric Culture?

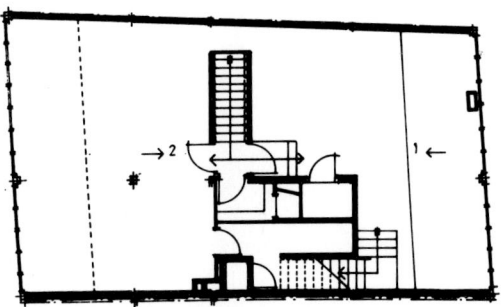

Third floor. Scale 1: 200

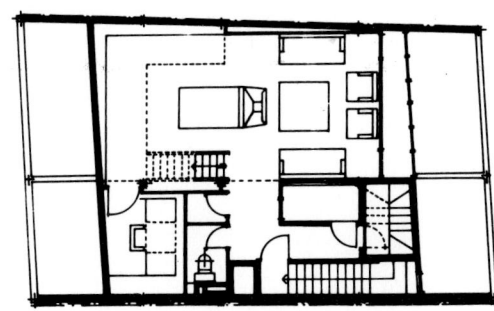

Fourth Floor

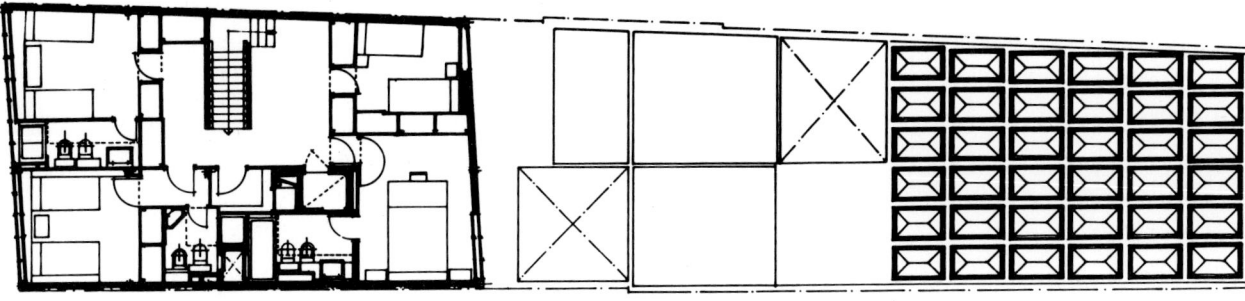

Second floor. Scale 1: 200

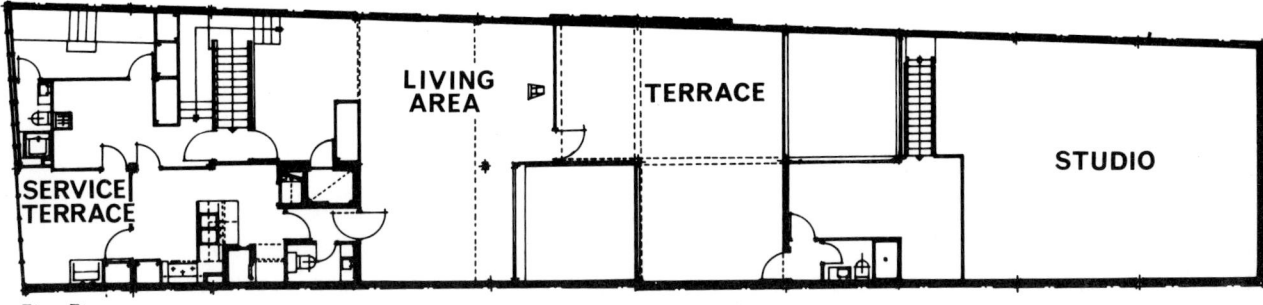

First Floor

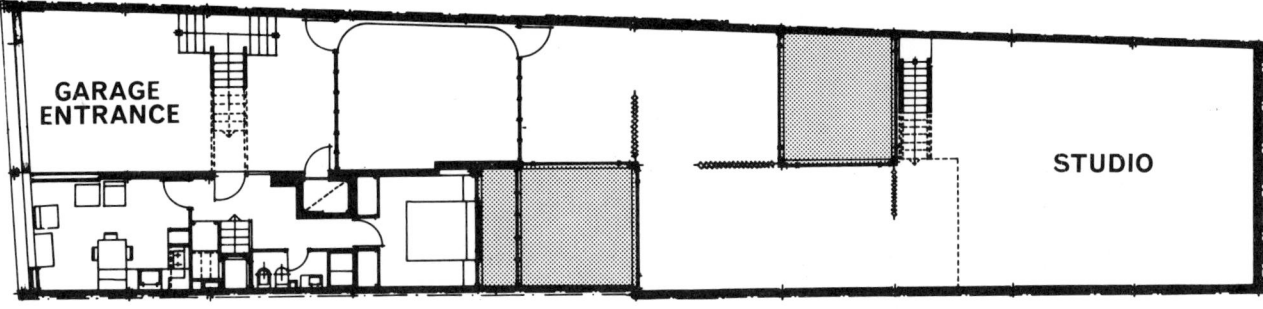

Ground Floor

3.2    Plan Scale 1: 230

While the major spaces and movement through them are correctly and subtly handled, the entrance sequence from the street to the living-room area tends to be a little too schematic and almost primitively handled. The first flight of stairs to the "front door" is out of scale with the exterior treatment of the entrance-garage and it's expected symbolic function of entry.

If a car is parked in the entrance, guests have an awkward route to the lift even if shown the way by the porter. This criticism may seem to be unnessarily pointed when the building is reasonably complete in its architectural objectives, but the problem of moving in and out of the built object is a recurrent failure to be found even in the best architecture.

3.4 The library. Note how the bookshelves are sunk into the wall thickness to maintain the continuous surface of the enclosing volume.

3.5 The enclosed garden terrace that links the living area with the studio.

3.3
The street façade. The central panels relate to the bedrooms, bathrooms, and terraces, according to the cill heights. The upper panels screen the childrens play court that runs through the house with the library "floating" above.
The details and proportions harmonise with the scale of the narrow street. (note that the upper panels are slightly higher to compensate the shortening effect of being further away, and to strike a longer note to conclude the upper limit of the compositon).

34

3.6 The lateral wall of the studio. Note the strong vertical rhythm sustained by alternating the white structural posts with the white plastic rainwater pipes. The order through confusing the identity of the elements is an interesting, if questionable, way of achieving a desired effect.

3.7 The entrance from the garage. The rear wall is a sliding door so that paintings can be moved easily in or out of the studio behind. The entrance staircase has an interior decorative treatment out of key with the rest of the space. Compare the plastered plinth with the brick-on-edge threshold of the porter's lodge on the right.

3.8 The plastic rooflight over the studio. Sculptural considerations claimed major importance over the climatic reality of heat transmission. The louvered screen would have been functionally better placed above the rooflights rather than below them, but the result would have been semantically confusing with the open areas.

3.9 The living room with terrace at lower level beyond. The outside is almost inside.

3.10 The studio with the gallery above that communicates with the house across the terrace.

# 4  CASA ROMEU Cadaqués. Province of Gerona
1961
ARCHITECTS: Alfonso Milá, Federico Correa
CLIENT: Industrialist, his wife (a sister of the architect Mila)
and eight children (4 boys, 4 girls)

## SITE
5.500 m² (6578 yd²) among the terraced olive groves above the fishing village of Cadaqués near the French frontier. Slopes NS.

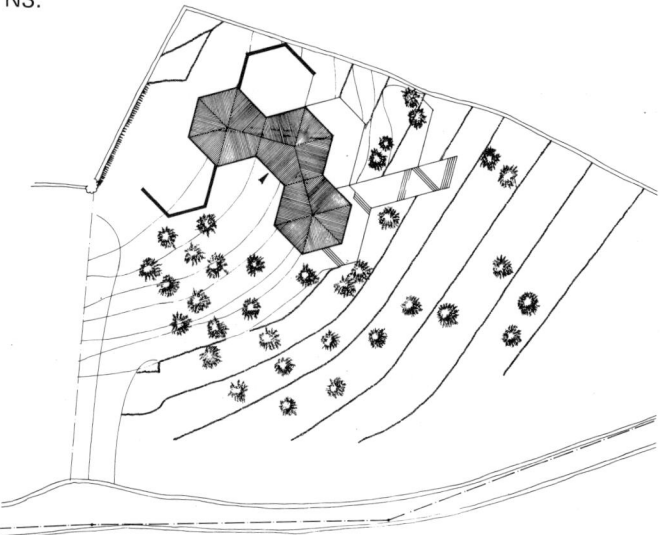

4.1    Site plan Scale 1:1000

## PLAN
A relatively large independent living area with boys' and girls' bedrooms on either side of a common-room which opens onto a semi-enclosed outside living area.

The parents suite lies inbetween the large living room and the rest of the house. A guest bedroom is accommodated between the childrens rooms and the parents rooms for either adult or child guests.

Kitchen and other service rooms placed to the N against the hill with their own service yard.

## CONSTRUCTION
Load-bearing stone walls with a well designed open timber truss and post system in the larger living unit.

## OBSERVATIONS
The dominance of form over function, with three engaged hexagonals, to reduce the volume to the scale of the stepped olive groves above the fishing village, acknowledges the realities of the geographical context. The repetition of the stonework of the fields and the simple volumetric effect achieved by the neat detailing of the continuous skin at the eaves and corners, ensure that the gesture of acknowledging historical realities in the context of modern architecture, are not lost. The break in the volume to form a covered terrace is more physical than visible, as the twin timber posts allow the eye to run around the outer skin without losing the hexagonal rhythm.

The fashionable vertical proportions of the fenestration are carried subtly from the individual wood windows and shutters of the bedrooms to the continuous thin metal frames of the living room.

If a poetic response is found in the reality of the building's exterior relationships, it has been lost inside the building where the internal distribution, and ones movement through it, bear little relation to the external form. Only in the main living room is the form legible from the inside. The repression of the awkward structure of the rest of the house, ingeniously disguised by expert decoration, contrasts incoherently with the dominant complexity of the living room, and is a weakness in the design.

4.2    Plan Scale 1:250

The use of stone so near the Mediterranean is a subversive challenge to the prolific consumer image of coastal architecture, a challenge that was spectacularly followed up by Salvador Dali, some five or six years later, when he intervened to stop the white-washing of the inland stone faces of the parish church of Cadaqués, in contrast to the white seaward façade.

4.3     View from the N with the service yard in the foreground and entrance court beyond.
        The use of hexagonal forms easily suggests the defined exterior spaces. Note that at the union of the hexagonals the tiled roof avoids a horizontal gutter by not following the logical form which would emphasize the difference between the three units. Instead, the designers have chosen to unite the building by joining the apex of each hexagonal with an undulating ridge. (see site plan).

4.4     View from the SE looking towards the living area. The sharp definition of the horizontal and vertical planes and their borders ensures a tight control of the prismatic form and its extension into the hill. Note the absence of parapet walls. The stepped olive groves grow into paved terraces that climb up through the outer living areas penetrating the invisible hexagonal skin to continue up into the womb of the home itself. The harmony and rhythm of cultivated nature have reached a poetic understanding with architecture.

4.5    View from the SW looking towards the living area. The continuity of the hexagonal form follows around the porch defined by the timber eaves, beam and corner posts.

4.6    View of the living area showing how the stepped levels of the dining, sitting, and porch, follow the slope of the hill. The trusses broken by the posts and beams can be clearly seen. This structural system, although logical in itself, is arbitrary in that simpler solutions of complete trusses without posts would have been just as correct technically: however the spatial effect of the topological and geometrical relations would have been different.

4.7 Perspective by the architect of the living area. The split-level and decorative effect of the complex broken structure are used to suggest different spatial parts without loss to the total environment.

4.8 View of the living area from the entrance hall. The sitting area is protected by being sunk below the dining area. The wide window cill is a continuation of the higher floor level.
Note the broken timber trusses. Structure can seldom be left exposed as a decorative element unless it is carefully detailed beyond the more technical necessities.

# 5 CASA CORREA Cadaqués. Province of Gerona
1962
ARCHITECTS: Alfonso Milá, Federico Correa
CLIENT: The architect himself

## SITE
Within the existing village fabric of closely packed houses and stepped streets.

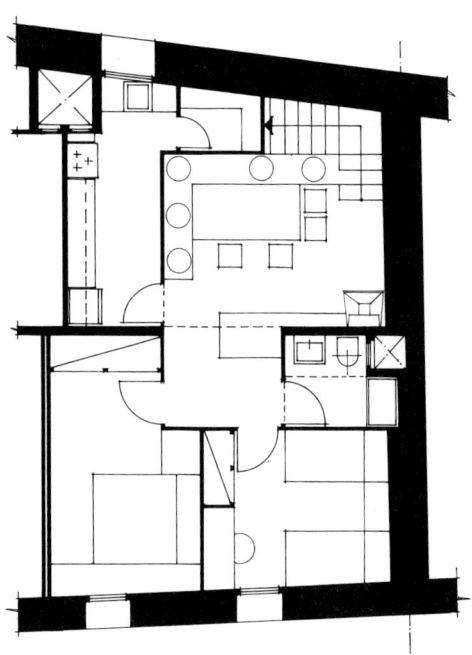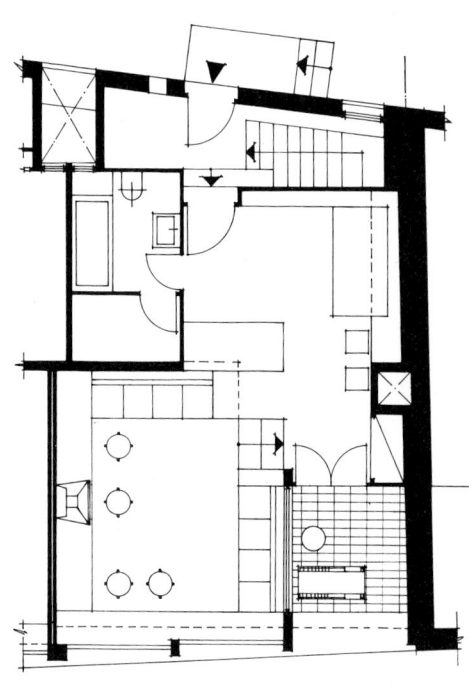

5.1    Plan Scale 1:140

## PLAN
Bed-living room with adjoining bathroom in one unit, 2-guest bedrooms, bathroom, dining-room and kitchen in another unit.

## OBSERVATIONS
Although a desirable environmental quality of a single living room may be achieved through the decorative effects of the finishes and the furnishings, (in spite of an apparent negative, or neutral, contribution of the architecture), it will nearly always remain superficial, in the true sense of the word, and incapable of absorbing and transmitting the full cultural content of an architectural space. Just how this is conveyed is easier to discover in an interior architectural design like Correa's bed-living room remodelled out of an old fishing-village house, than perhaps when the interior forms part of a designed architectural whole.

Apart from working and washing, this sleeping and living space is open to nearly every possible kind of activity from the solitary to the kaleidoscopic rivalry of a Cadaqués summer social evening. At the same time the sophistication of the architectural vocabulary had to lie within the grammatic simplicity of a vernacular architecture tempered by successive fashionable breezes that drift up and down the Mediterranean coast every summer.

The pitched ceiling divides the room into two basic parts, the inner space, which is entered first, and the outer space with its view of the village and port. This outer area, is further divided into three sub-areas, the sunken sitting area, the enclosed terrace, and a fluid intermediate area which is an extension and link between these two sub-areas and the inner space.

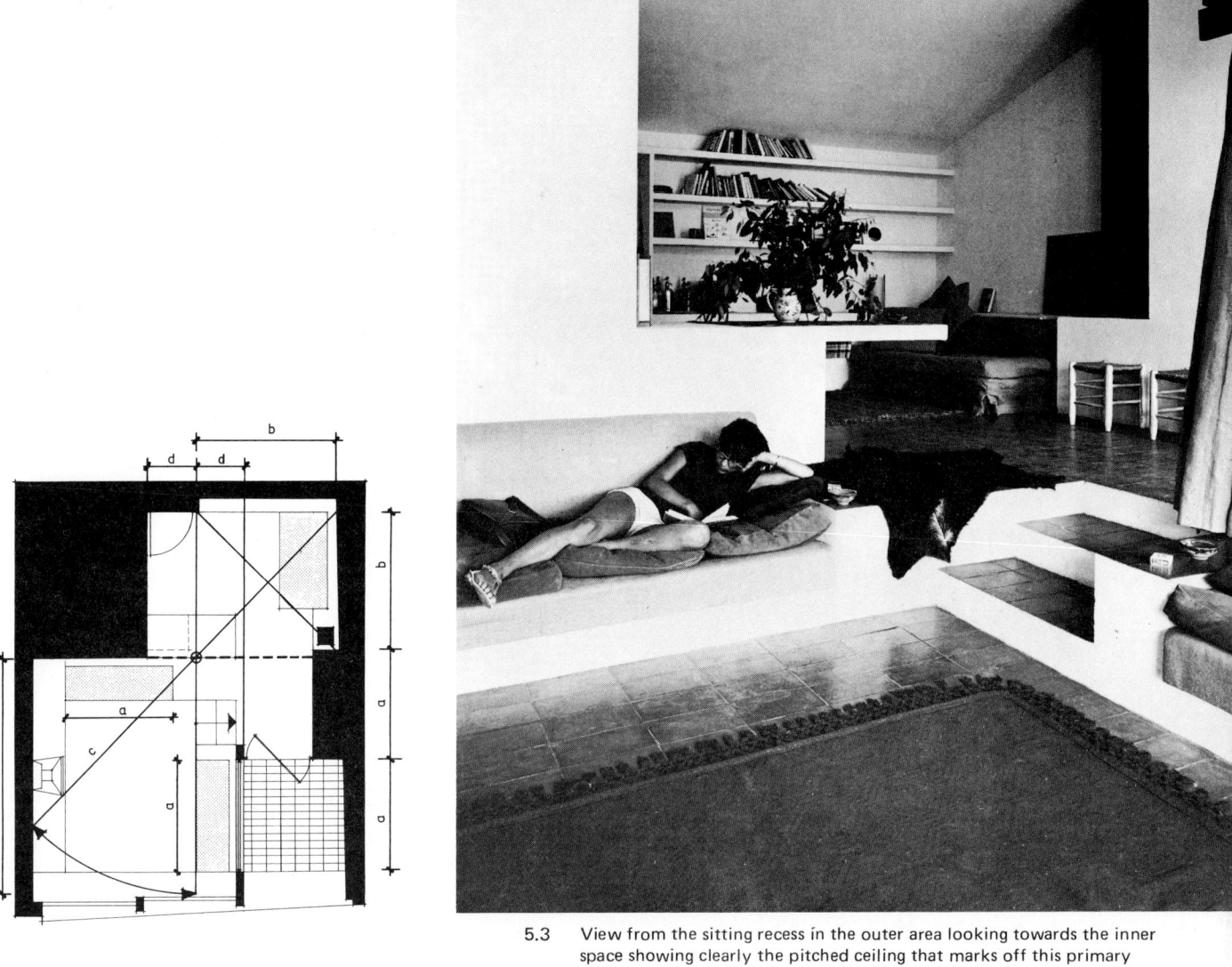

5.2    Diagram Scale 1: 140

5.3    View from the sitting recess in the outer area looking towards the inner space showing clearly the pitched ceiling that marks off this primary division of the room into two areas. The built-in table that is the generator around which the inter-related sub-spaces revolve can be clearly seen in the middle. Note the edge of the solid support which is cut back to coincide with the point where the diagonal lines of the sub-spaces as shown on the geometrical plan analysis.

The real poetic content of this complex space lies in the relationship of its parts to each other and to the whole and in the agreeable ambiguity of undefined situations.

An analysis of the plan shows the geometrical relationship, although this does not necessarily mean that this was the method of design, for free creation often prefers to be intuitive. However the analysis does indicate how this ambiguous relationship has been achieved and where its generative point is located. It is the built-in table which grows out of the wall that divides the two primary spaces and that blocks the entrance axis to enclose the sunken sitting area. This table deflects the movement through the room from the entrance axis onto the visual axis that is drawn out through the terrace. Immediately the sunken pit of the sitting area with its chimney is revealed! The surprise of the picturesque is almost complete. However a new

spatial dimension is discovered when sitting down in the pit from the low visual level that is given when looking back into the inner space.

The canons of the International Style have not been rejected, but have been enriched by the contrast of the introduction of a movement along a broken asymmetrical axis (a Spanish invariant) through the quiet, articulated cubic Mediterranean space.

5.4    View of the semi-enclosed terrace with the
       harbour of Cadaqués beyond.

5.5    View from the intermediate area that links
       the terrace and the sitting space as well as
       the entrance and bed space behind. The view
       of the village along the deflected axis
       through the terrace can be appreciated as
       well as the surprise view of the sitting area
       and chimney.

5.6    View of the dining area located on the floor
       below the bed-living room. Note the sharp
       surface treatment of the mass.

# 6 CASA LUCIO Torrelodones. Madrid
1962
ARCHITECT: Fernando Higueras
CLIENT: Husband and wife, who are two painters and their
four children

## SITE
9.200 m² (2¼ acres) somewhat isolated site in the arid stony scrubland to the N of Madrid. Steep NS slope.

6.1    Site plan Scale 1: 1000

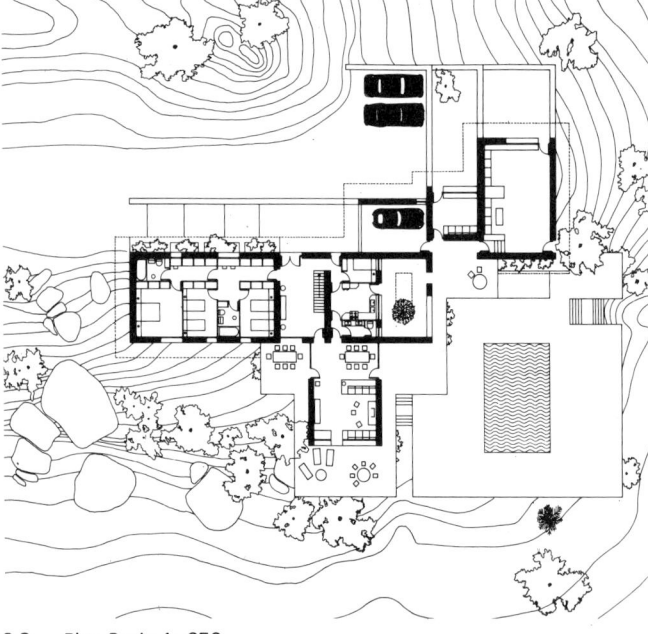

6.2    Plan Scale 1: 650

## PLAN
The distribution of the rooms follow the now classic Frank Lloyd Wright's Unity Church plan-diagram of two wings separately articulated and joined with a see-through entrance link.

The garage and the two studios are attached as an appendix in a series of compartments staggered around the ridge of the hill to close off the entrance approach.

The enclosing stone walls follow a differentiated articulation that destroys the plan-diagram to establish a second hierarchy of spatial relationships between the elements of the plan.

The double pitched roof that swings back and forth along a single, broken, asymmetrical axis destroys the legibility of the two previous orders to dominate the final composition itself.

The horizontal eaves and cantilevered terraces introduce a fourth compositional order of a series of staggered platforms hovering over the bouldered scrubland as though hardly daring to disturb the eternity of nature.

A pierced terrace holds the swimming pool within the outer angle of the house as it turns around the hill.

## CONSTRUCTION
Stone load-bearing walls, prestressed concrete beams and joists, tiled roof.

## OBSERVATIONS
The legible, formal result that would normally follow the distribution plan-diagram has been systematically erased to make way for a series of imposed, superior, formal orders. This has been done by running the enclosing walls of the bedroom wing through the entrance link to incorporate the kitchen and service court to form a rigid rectangle that effectively destroys the articulated distribution. On the other hand, an artificial link is forced between the entrance and living area by separating the enclosing walls of the latter to form a pause in a see-through dining area that acts as a visual link between the E and W terraces. The break is further emphasized by raising the ceiling at this point. The imposition of one formal order on another creates an ambiguous relationship between the elements which, if controlled and dominated by the architect, leads to a rich complexity of space but, if weakly handled, to an anarchic confusion of a bad plan. In the case of the *Casa Lucio* the situation is dominated by the addition of two more sets of formal orders, the irregular pendulum flow of the pitched roof that beats its own rhythm independently of the compartments below, and the successive flight of decks frozen in an irregular formation as they brush over the dropping hillside. The most interesting feature of the design of the roof, in defiance of the plan, is the audacious use of stone gables that defy the accepted principles of gravity. The reason for this break of the accepted codes is the same that Gaudi and Berenguer chose in the construction of Bellesguard (pebble stone rainwater pipes) that is, an unremitting overall use of one or two materials to give unity to an otherwise complex form. The reason behind this complex superimposition of sets of formal orders lies in the relationship of the built object to the site. The fragile intention of not disturbing the holy virginity of the site has led to the virtual disappearance of the building submerged into the hill as one approaches the house. Only the

horizontal shadows under the broad sweep of the eaves indicate something other than a primitive rural construction. It is these shadows that are picked up and scattered beneath the building by the cantilevered platforms as the hill falls away to the S on the other side.

The *Casa Lucio* seems a far cry from the International Style (not to mention Mies van der Rohe), and in the architects use of old roof tiles, an old ship's boarding for the floor as well as the exposed factory-produced concrete beams he deliberately provokes the question of the building's validity within the modern movement. If the answer is affirmative then the partial incorporation of a vernacular vocabulary is a sign of the movement's maturity.

6.3     View of the house from the SE; the two studios are on the right, the living area is in the centre with the bedroom wing behind.
Note the part played by the partially covered court, with the lone cypress, in providing an excuse for a wider link in the flowing roof from the house to the studios.

6.4    View from the S. The underside of the decks that support the terraces and roof display the identical exposed
       construction. The almost invisible railing does nothing to distract the similarity between the eaves and the other
       platforms. The effect of hovering just over the scrub creates a fragile but dramatic relationship between the
       architecture and the natural state of the site.

6.5, 6.6    The two photographs show the clear intention of the literal identification of the house with the site through the mixed use of natural and manufactured materials in their intrinsic state. The steel ring beam that runs around the edge of the roof slab has been left to oxidise under a varnish. The poetic simplicity seems to echo the rigour of Castille.

# 7  CASA BALLBE  Avda. N. Sra. de Lourdes, Pedralbes. Barcelona
## 1963
ARCHITECTS:   Enric Tous and Josep M. Fargas
CLIENT:   Businessman with wife and two boys 16 and 17.

## SITE
5.000 m² (1¼ acre) on a rough hillside overlooking, to the SE
the wealthy residential suburb built around the 14th century
monastery of Pedralbes, N to S slope with access road on the
S and E boundaries.

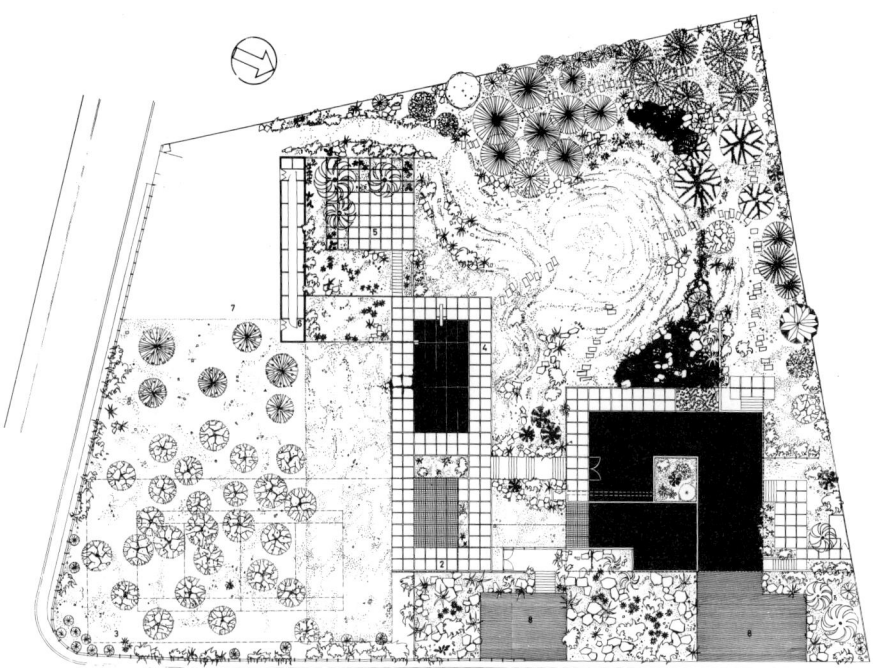

7.1    Site plan Scale 1:830

## PLAN
1.25 x 1.25m (4 x 4ft) module-planned house on two and a
half floors using industrially manufactured components with a
2.50m (8.2ft) plus structural steel grid.

Paralysis of the owner required a design for wheel-chair circulation planned on the first floor to enjoy the fine views over
Barcelona. A lift connects the garage porch below with this
floor.

The first floor contains the principal bedroom suite, living
areas and service rooms which, because of the slope of the site,
lead easily onto the service court.

In the centre of the house are two 5 x 5m (16 x 16ft) wells, one
with a profusion of plants and open to the sky, and the other
with a staircase connecting the lower floor living-area for the
teenage boys, with the upper living area for the parents.

Adjoining this lower living-room are two independent apart-
ments, one for the sons and the other for guests.

Below is a garden room and mechanical services.

7.2    Basement Plan Scale 1: 250

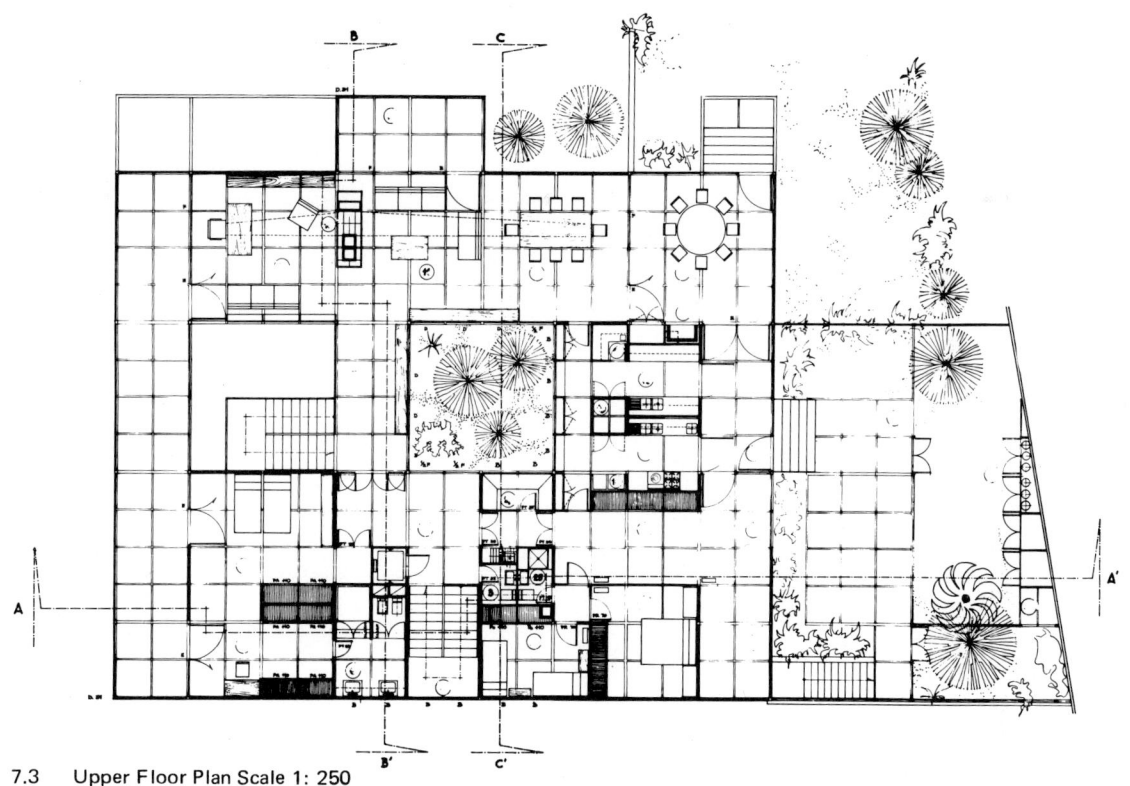

7.3    Upper Floor Plan Scale 1: 250

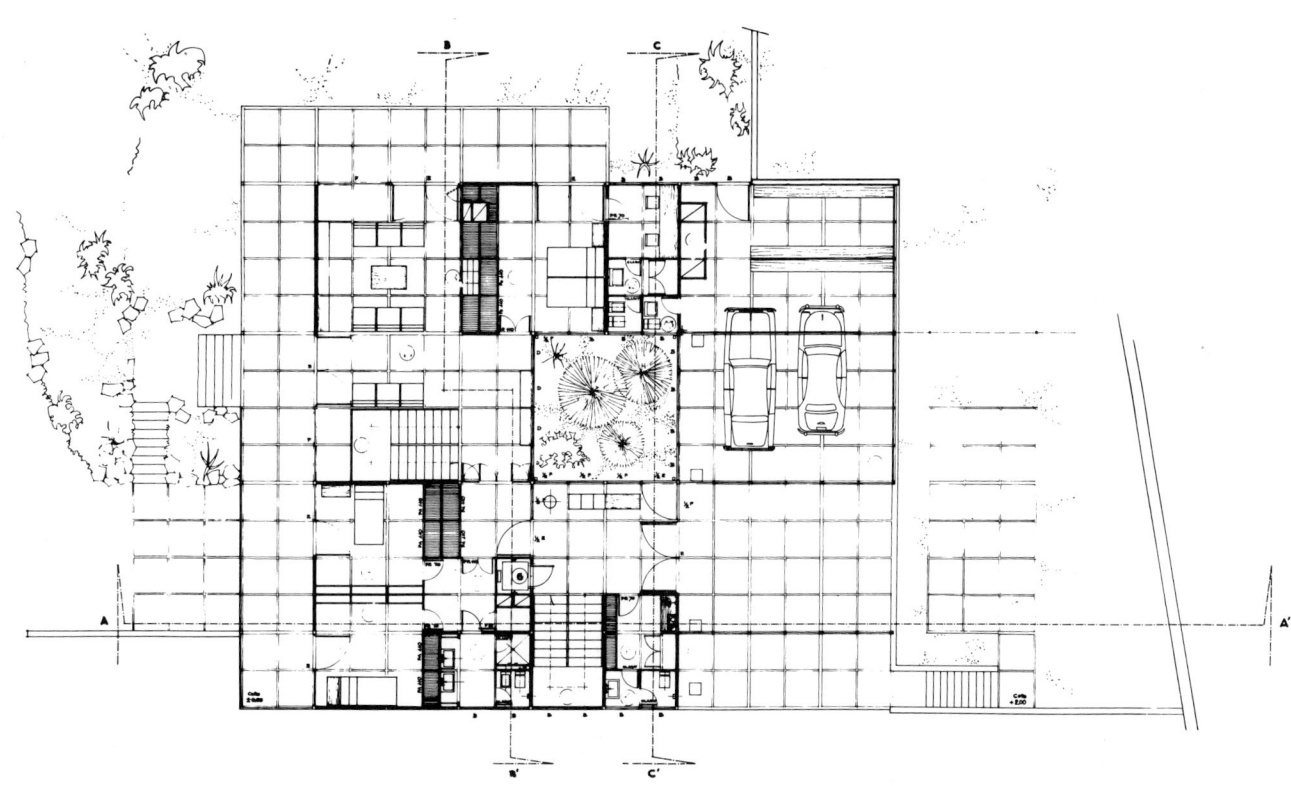

7.4    Lower Floor Plan Scale 1: 250

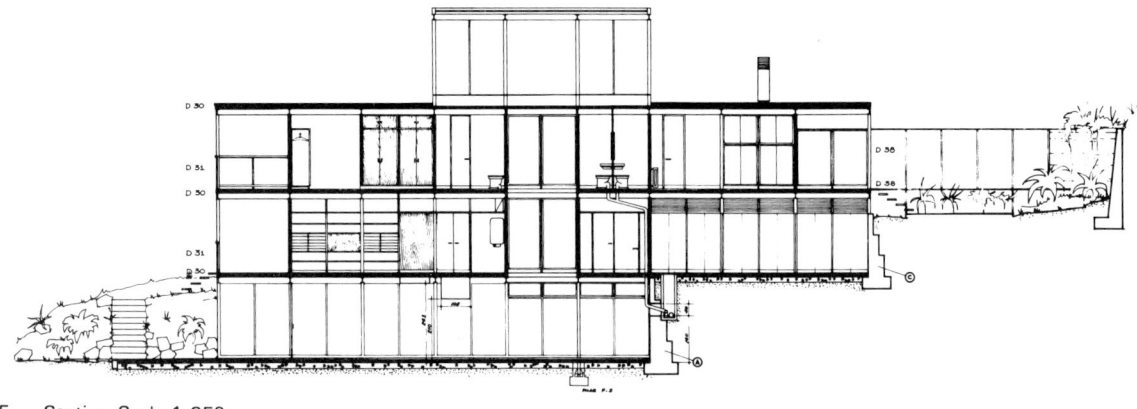

7.5    Section Scale 1:250

7.6    The E and entrance façade. The symmetrical composition of solids and voids is broken by the wide porch of the garage. The expression of the central staircase that runs through the three floors is surprisingly suppressed on the ground floor and base-ment façade components. The constant image of the steel structural support over small and wide spans create doubt as to the technological efficiency of the system.

7.7    The N façade, containing the kitchen, laundry and other service rooms, from the service court. In spite of, or perhaps because of, the artisan methods of industrial production and assembly, the detailing is superbly consistent and well thought out.

## CONSTRUCTION

Metal frame structure, and sub-structure with glass or asbestos cement and wood sandwich panels, hollow clay-tile floor slabs with fired clay floor tile finish.

## OBSERVATIONS

When architectural values have to give way to the dominance of one special objective, there is little room for an interesting play of topological relationships. The built object suffers in being oversimple and leaves an arid ground for imaginative, poetic intuition. The *Casa Ballbe* suffers in this respect in being too schematic and prison-like in its faithful adherence to an imposed module of components that throbs its way through every room and open space with tireless monotony.

The interesting contradiction is a losing battle between archi-tecture and technology, and the architects have used the result for constructing a transient technological experiment with a redundancy value. The fact that the owner, with his specialised living requirements, died just after the completion of his dream house, which has now been partly taken down and converted into two independent homes, seems to justify the architects foresight. The economic, social situation in Spain indicates otherwise. A technological experiment is only valuable socially if it is carried out in order to gain experience of a new product which, if successful, is then made available on the market. The mass extension of the *Casa Ballbe* typology is doubtful in Spain. Abundant manufacture of quality components at an economic cost does not exist, nor is there any demand for it at present. Looking beyond national frontiers, technological prototypes are better built where previous experience and a sufficient market is available.

As for the fluidity of changing needs, traditional housing can be adapted as well or even better since a change of decorative style or just fashion, can be easily applied. On the other hand where the built object is of such total architectural value as Philip Webb's Red House, Bexley Heath, nothing is lost by its being occupied by three or four families instead of William Morris and his wife Jane Burden, for whom it was built.

In the end, the question must remain open, for history to decide in each case if the projected values were sufficient to meet the real ones.

7.8 The W façade. The large roof overhang responds to the climatic conditions of solar protection from the afternoon sun. The Japanese style is obviously intentional with the underlying treatment afforded to the garden. Even technology is subject to style.

7.9 The main living room with the staircase that leads down to the boys' living area on the left. The spectacular ruthless simplicity reminds one of Richard Neutra's Hollywood modern environments.

7.10 The kitchen. The catalytic rhythm of the dominating module is felt everywhere.

# 8 CASA SANTONJA  c. del Grillo de Pozuelo de Alarcon. Somosaguas: Madrid
1964
ARCHITECTS:  Fernando Higueras, Antonio Miró
CLIENT: Civil engineer and his wife

## SITE
2.537 m² (3034 yd²) adjoining the nearby natural park *Casa de Campo* on the crest of one of the rolling hills that form the rather bleak surrounding plains to the North of Madrid, but commanding extensive views.

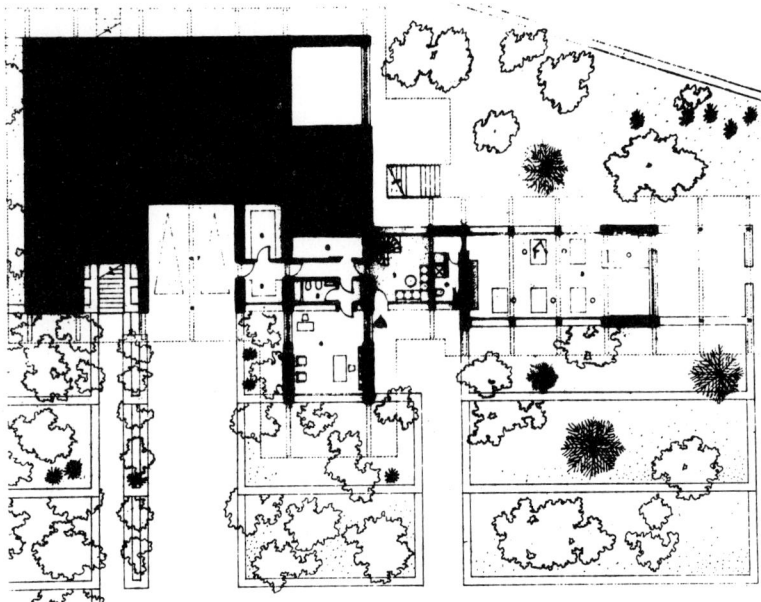

8.1    Site Plan Scale 1: 400

## THE PLAN
The distribution follows the same articulated plan-diagram of the *Casa Lucio* (No. 6) with a see-through entrance link between the bedroom wing and living areas. The entrance, however, is designed to be effected from below rising up by spiral staircase into the link space.

As in the *Casa Lucio* the formal order of the distribution is subjected to the imposition of additional compositional orders. The living area is continued through an L-shaped kitchen that breaks the longitudinal generative axis of the house. This living area is also extended at right angles to this axis with a court to the NW shielded by a porch. (This has now been converted into a guest bedroom). This produces a cruciform plan.

The double pitched roof swings back and forth along the generative axis related more to the profile of the built object and the continuity of its own surface, rather than the formal structural organisation of the house itself.

The repeated horizontal lines of the eaves and cantilevered terraces over the low stepped ziggurat introduces another important compositional order.

## CONSTRUCTION
Load-bearing stone walls; mixed timber and steel beams supporting a tiled roof.

## OBSERVATIONS
This is a further development of the architectural vocabulary used by Higueras in the *Casa Lucio* — the limited selection and intrinsic use of materials (though this discipline is not extended to installations), the superimposed compositional orders, the decorative use of the structural system, and the paradoxical floating submergence of the house-site relationship.

The canons of architectural propriety are more violently broken: with the introduction of false structural timber beams between the steel sandwich joists used when the span is too great for timber alone; with structural stone walls perched on top of timber beams (a steel plate does the trick); with an over complex roof that rises up in the centre to enclose only the upper half of an open court; and finally with the continuity of the swinging roof achieved by the breaking of its own order, of two constant cantilevers, to widen the eaves on either side of the living room so that it does not coincide with the 'correct' width over the porch behind. This last item is obviously within the legitimate right of any artist to break his own rules, but the weakness lies in the small measure — hardly 500mm (20in).

The monumental effect of raising the house upon a low ziggurat is in part justified in order to hide (submerge) the lower floor reserved for a future drawing office. However, the formal wish to cast a repetition of strong horizontal lines to establish

a mutual affinity between the built object and the site was
obviously intended as well. Although this abuse of the normal
code of architectural compositional honesty is disquietening,
the resulting effect is an intriguing volumetric balance, and a
stimulating spatial experience within and around the house that
at the same time never loses control of its quiet, human
dimensions.

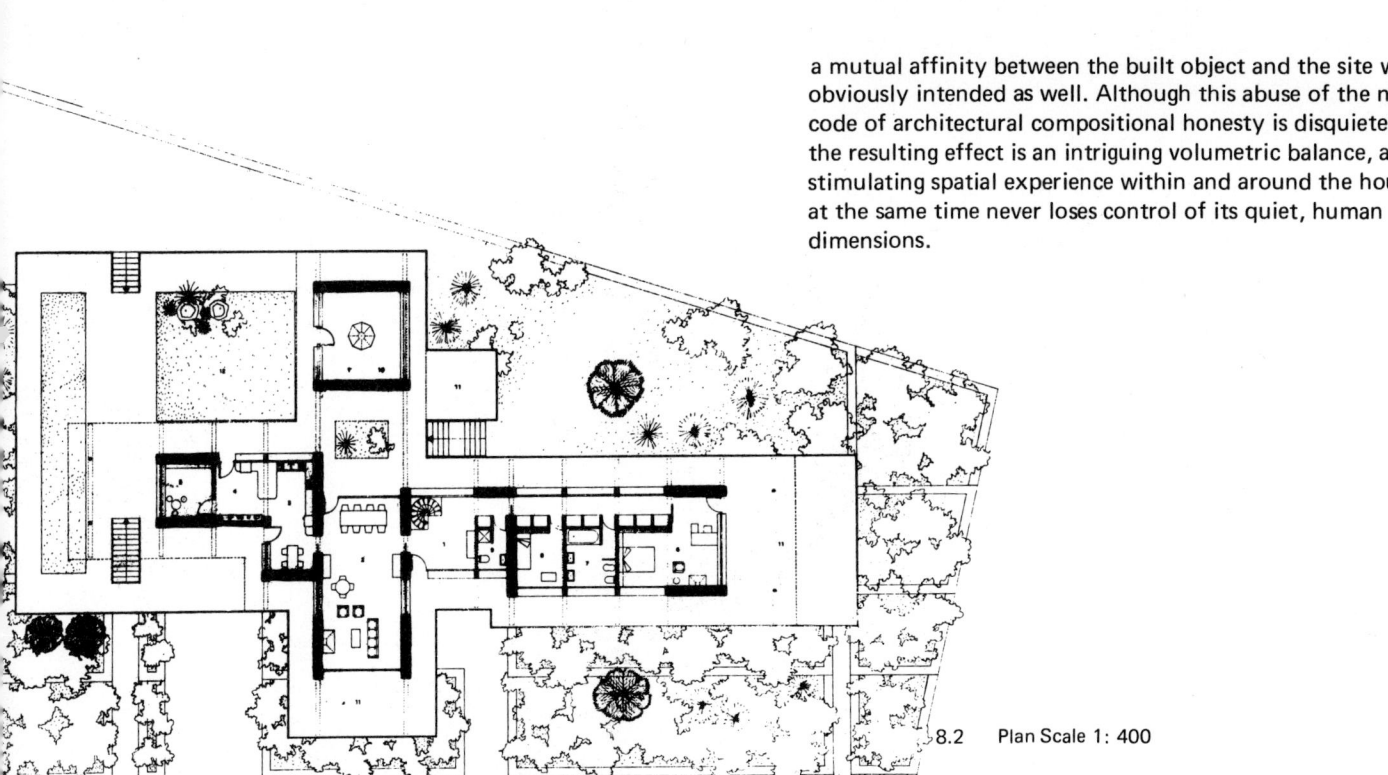

8.2    Plan Scale 1: 400

8.3    Section Scale 1: 200

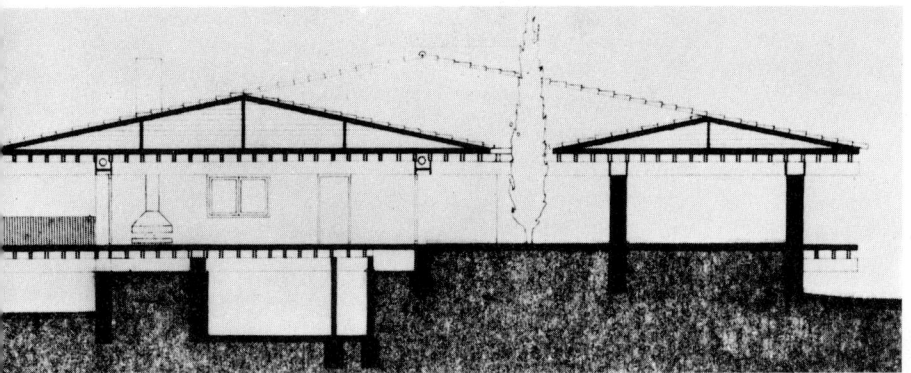

8.4    View from the SE. The living room is in
       the centre with the kitchen on the left
       and bedrooms beyond on the right. The
       slight break in the gable over the living-
       room in order to maintain the continuous
       flow of the roof is just visible.

8.5 The entrance to the house from **E**. The repetitive horizontal lines identify the house with the total architectonic treatment of the site.

8.6 View from the S towards the living area with the kitchen on the left. The tiled floor of the deck indistinctly passes over the solid and void below unifying the platform with the similar varnished tiled floor within the house.

8.7 The living room with the dining area and beyond, the court with the porch wall sealing off the heat of the afternoon sun. To the left an open sliding-door allows the free flow of space, and use, between the kitchen and the rest of the living area.
The quiet human scale given by the continuous 2 m (6ft 6in) high horizontal line of the underside of the timber and steel structure, repeats a favourite device of Frank Lloyd Wright.

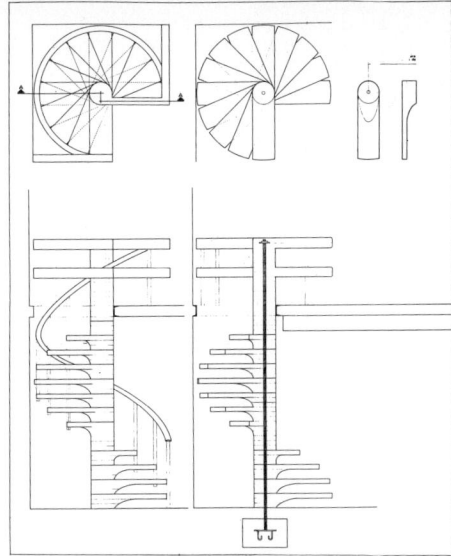

8.8    Plans and section of spiral staircase.

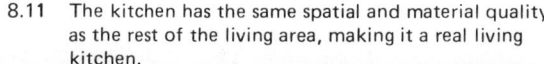

8.9    The timber spiral staircase with its curved cantilever from the central pole contrasting with the sharp rectangular style of the rest of the house.

8.10   The main bedroom with its long train-like corridor that connects it to the entrance hall. Note the consistent 2 m high horizontal line.

8.11   The kitchen has the same spatial and material quality as the rest of the living area, making it a real living kitchen.

# 9  CASA MILA  c. de los Somatenes. Esplugas de Llobregat. Barcelona
## 1965
ARCHITECTS:  Alfonso Milá. Federico Correa.
CLIENT:  Lawyer, his wife and five children (3 girls, 2 boys)

SITE
In private, pine-covered grounds where the architects had built
an earlier house, to the SW of Barcelona, just off the main road
to Madrid. Slopes NW—SE.

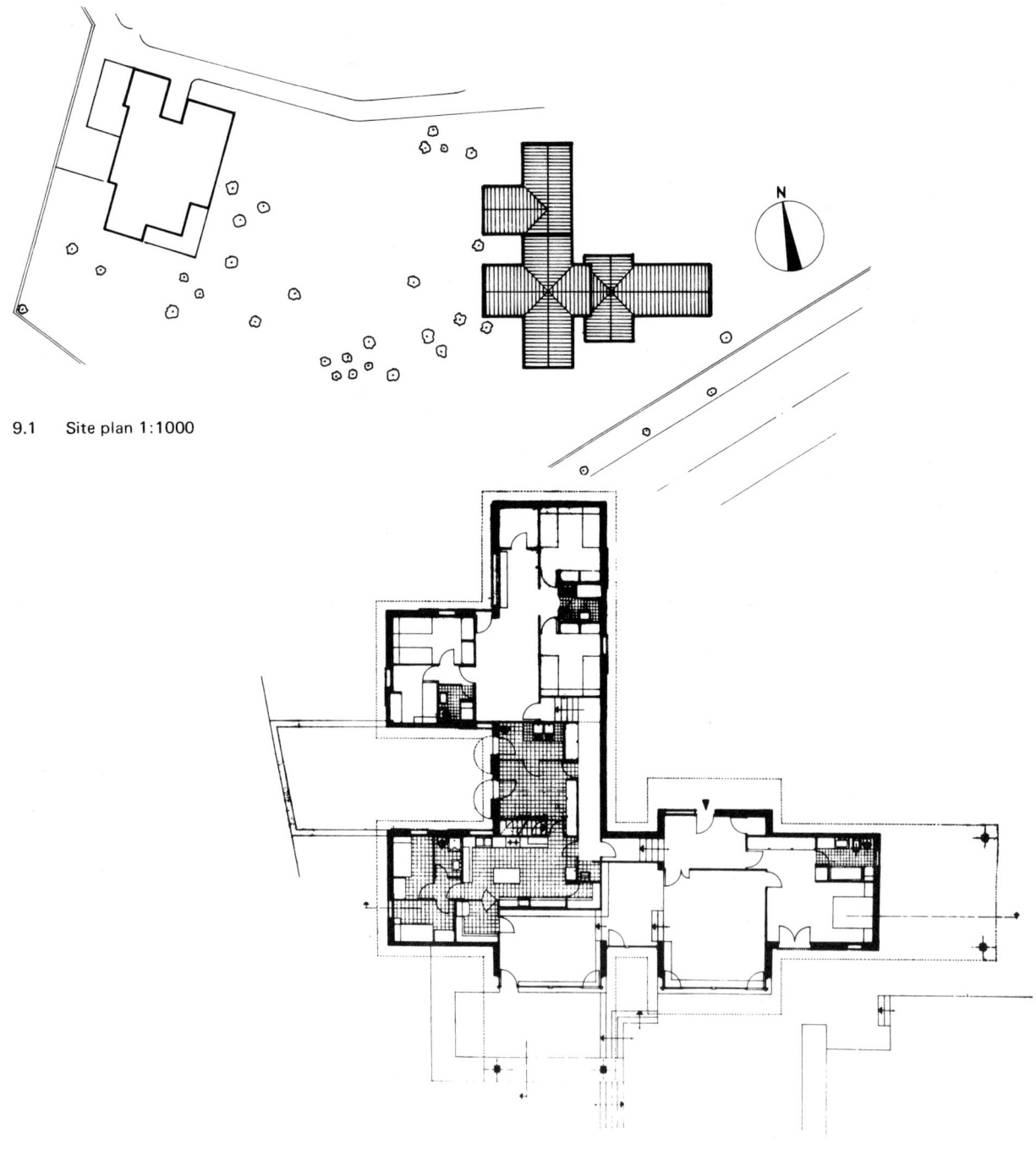

9.1    Site plan 1:1000

9.2    Plan 1:333

## PLAN

The large living area is formally sub-divided into sitting and dining sections, with a small library-games area between them. The dining section has a large porch for outdoor meals.

The principal bedroom suite is attached to the E of the sitting area, the roof of which is unexpectedly extended to provide a sheltered car port.

To the W of the living area there is an L-shaped domestic service section containing kitchen, laundry and servants' rooms.

To the N of the service section is another L-shaped wing with two self-contained double bedroom and bathroom units for the children. These give access to a common play area.

Between the angles of the service and children's sections there is a small, walled, service patio.

## CONSTRUCTION

Load-bearing brick walls support a tiled pitched roof that maintains a constant 6m (20ft) span throughout the building providing a basic structural module.

## OBSERVATIONS

The same inconsistency between the interior planning and external volume found in the same architects' *Casa Romeu* is again evident in this curious suburban house. It appears inconsistent because the architects evidently decided to create a volumetric interest by dividing the three sections, childrens wing, central service area, living and parents wing, into distinct levels following the natural slope of the ground, but then failed to maintain this clarity by merging the living areas into the adjoining service volume. This weakness of definition is apparent externally, too, as can be seen clearly in the aerial photograph where the pitched roof overlaps itself in all directions. Weak definition does have the positive quality of ambiguity or even complexity, as Venturi has so rightly pointed out, but the integrity of the architectural whole must be maintained if a poetic level is to be achieved. In the absence of this the superb succession of broken spaces that form the living areas of this house remain in the realm of decorative effects.

The house is curious for its tropical, one might almost say, missionary, architectural character, genuinely inspired perhaps by the vegetation and climate of the site which is aggravated by the small rural scale of the assembled broken volumes that make up the house. The restrained use of brick and the primi-

9.3 View from the N of the entrance court with the children's wing on the right.
The position of the entrance with its protective porch is a little forced and its lost relationship with the car port seems to be a missed opportunity to create a strong composition.

9.4 The three distinct sections of the house can be identified rising in clockwise direction as the parents' bedroom and living area, central service area, and the childrens' bedroom area. The simple drop between the childrens' wing and the service area is not repeated with the same clarity between the service area and living section where the overlapping pitches are confusing.

tive handling of the concrete beams and trusses certainly break the expected code for this type of building, but one is led to consider whether the breaking of the established code of identification on its own is an exclusive property of the vanguardists or whether it can also be a reflective, in a minor, positive sense, step backwards?

59

9.5 View from the S with the dining porch in the foreground and
the car port at the extreme right.
The primitive structural details contrast strongly with the refined
interior decoration and it is this contradiction, which is intentional, that gives a lively interest to the building. However the
strong white horizontal bands over the windows unnecessarily
disturb the point of contact between the two.

9.6 View of the dining porch looking W.
The rural structure with its broad eaves seems a far cry from the
International Style that launched the modern movement upon
the world in earnest in the 'twenties. The revolt against its
simple vocabulary in the 'fifties and 'sixties opened the
possibility of investigating the incorporation of traditional
and vernacular language. If this investigation is to avoid
being merely archaeological it must be placed in a critical context.
In the honest use of brick, concrete, and tile, the architects
have shown that an interesting complement to form can be
obtained even though the risk of losing the 'soul' of architecture
is great.

9.7 The living area looking towards the library and games area with the dining area beyond. The procession of successive spaces is well articulated by the use of different floor levels, ceiling heights, and the broken skin of the containing walls.

9.8 The dining area seen from the library and games' corner. Note the subtle connection of the continuous ceiling between the two parts otherwise defined by the broken wall and floor surfaces.

# 10  CASA CARNER  Tartera, Das. La Cerdanya, Province of Gerona
## 1965
ARCHITECT:  Manuel Ribas
CLIENT:  Businessman, wife and ten year old son

## SITE
8.000 m² (2 acre) slightly sloping plot in an estate development
in the Pyrenees designed by the same architect on the *Radburn*
principle. Each plot has a pre-selected area where the house has
to be sited. No boundary walls are permitted.

## PLAN
The house was built for the long summer vacations when the
NE wind and strong afternoon sun from the W were the main
climatic problems. This inspired an open L-shaped plan around
a porch for sheltered exterior living.

The volume of the building has been given a mega-form that is
a slice of a hexagonal prism. The particular functions have been
subordinated to this formal "whole" that retains the scale of
the traditional constructions of La Cerdanya. The three floors
are each split into two levels; the lowest contains a double
garage, the kitchen and dining room; on the next floor the main
living-room, entrance, and porch; half a floor up are the bedrooms. Under the roof are the guest rooms, and finally a large
loft.

## CONSTRUCTION
Mixed structure of load-bearing stone walls, and concrete
columns, supporting a timber-trussed slate roof.

## OBSERVATIONS
The marked difference between the clear, primary mega-form
designed for a correct scale with the landscape, and the subsequent loose design of the micro-form disappoints first
expectations. The large volume and enormous porch arouse an
interest that collapses with the unsympathetic treatment of
surface, corners, protruding prow of the S facade, balcony
railings, odd entrance lobby afterthought, and ambiguous roof
structure, that together form a collection of heterogeneous,
details that seem to destroy the generous scale of the
whole.

The breakaway from the right angle is always an exciting event
with its complex spatial possibilities within a small building,
but the alien planning problems it creates have to be very carefully worked out. The awkward left-over shapes in the interior
distribution, especially the living room, indicate that this self-

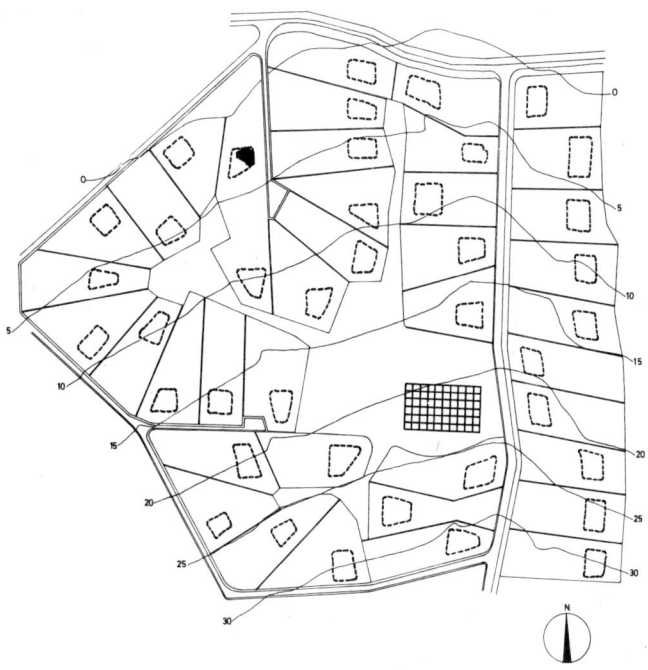

10.1   Site Plan Scale 1: 10,000

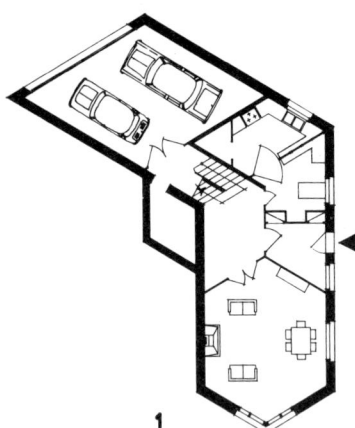

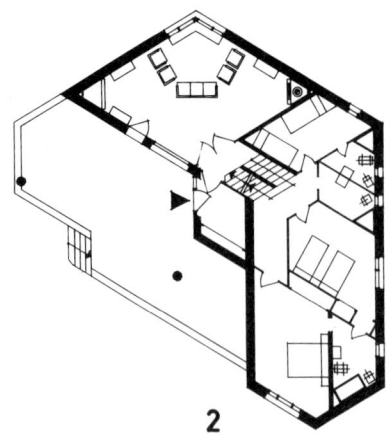

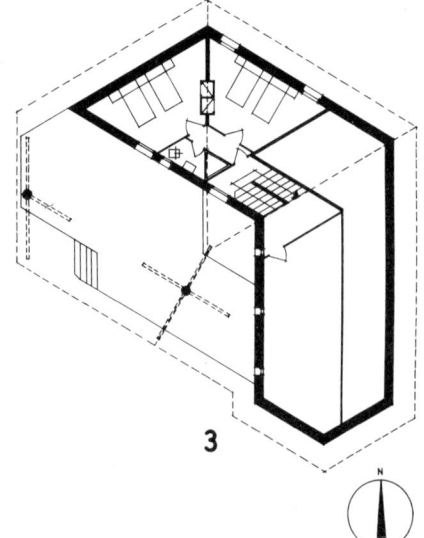

10.2   Plan Scale 1:333

10.3    View of the house from the N. The large scale hexagonal mega-form is the
        dominant compositional element. The dominance of mass over void assists
        this primary image, as does the angle window that links one plane to another.
        Unfortunately the large ordered cornerstones destroy the effect of a continuous
        skin by framing the planes into panels.

imposed problem has not been successfully solved.

However, with all its failings and, precisely because of them,
the building is a clear didactic example of the different roles
and contradictions of mega-and and micro-form. A successful
fusion obscures the reality beneath this generative creative
decision of a primary selection in favour of one or other mega-
form types. The rest of the composition should both compli-
ment and extend the rules of the original idea.

10.4    The strong image of the roof structure over the porch is incongruous only
        because of its isolation from the stone load-bearing wall system. The structure
        itself is crude but not out of place in the primitive spirit with which the whole
        built object has been treated, but the failure to integrate the design within the
        whole, disturbs the unity of the building. The cut-back of the roof would have
        been better omitted.
        The high porch admits the low Winter sun while retaining an adequate protection
        in the Summer.

10.5    The concrete pillar and timber
        roof structure is a bold
        attempt to break the
        vernacular language while
        retaining the spirit of its
        spacious dimensions.

# 11 CASA VILASECA Can Bordoi. Llinás. Province of Barcelona

1965

ARCHITECTS: Josep M. Martorell, Oriol Bohigas,
David Mackay

CLIENT: Family: lawyer, wife and five girls (aged 6—17)

## SITE

Large private estate adjoining existing farm buildings on a pass through pine-forested hills between the Montseny massive and the coast just ½ hour by car to the NE of Barcelona. W—E slope.

and/or small groups of people at the same time and allow a certain free relationship between them, permitting an easy movement from one group to another. It is an environment as suitable for the individual as for sixty persons.

There is also a formal dining area and an intermediate space between this and the kitchen for informal meals and other domestic activities.

The terraces of the principal floor coincide with the level of the farm track that turns around the house on the W side. The upper floor contains the bedrooms and overlooks the living space below. On the W side are four double cabins with shared bathrooms; on the S side the principal bedroom suite and on the E side two guest bedrooms each with its own bathroom. A small linen room completes the program.

Below the principal floor is a small self-contained one bedroom flat and study for guests, and a large communal dormitory for whole groups of guests (usually young people). There is a large garage which also houses some of the farm vehicles.

11.1   Site plan Scale 1: 1200

## PLAN

The house is sited so that it becomes part of, and completes, the existing group of buildings. The volume and facades of the outer envelope is related in scale to this pre-existing built environment while the interior is freed to formalise the spatial necessities of the program and the relations between its parts.

A steel structure with 5m x 5m (16ft x 16ft) bays establishes the basic frame which relates, without governing, the interior and exterior divisions.

The principal floor, reached by a flight of steps which turn around an open court between the new and the existing buildings, consists of a large complex of inter-related spaces These eddy around an undefined centre to accommodate large

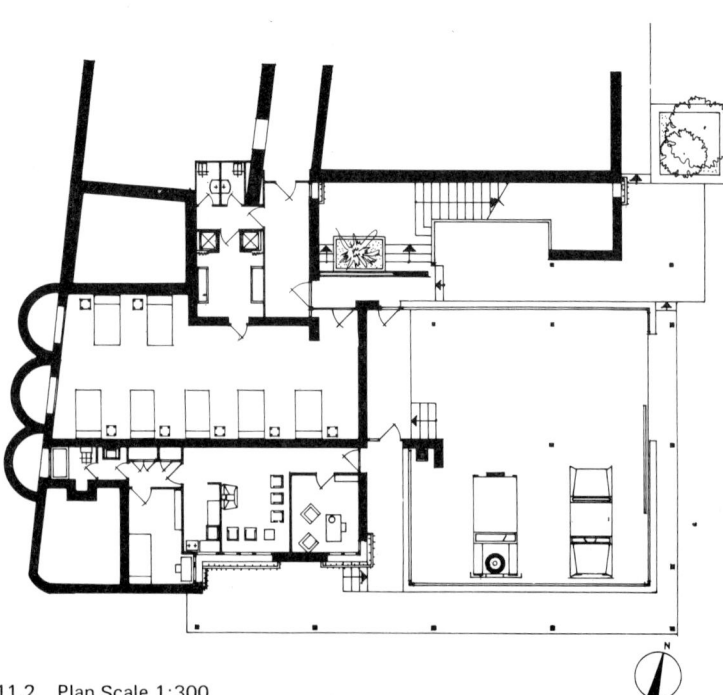

11.2   Plan Scale 1:300

## CONSTRUCTION
Steel-frame structure and floors, tiled external walls and floors, timber ceiling, pitched tile roof.

## OBSERVATIONS
This large country house had an unusual program in that the owners, with growing extensive socio-cultural relations and five children, required the house to be open to friends and visitors alike, and that this character should be translated into architectural terms.

Three *a priori,* fundamental decisions were taken by the architects before the detailed analysis and solution of the program.

1. To site the house so that it became part of the existing group of buildings, even though this entailed the demolition of a barn recently restored by the owners. As Denys Lasdun once remarked, design is divided between the dialectic with the pencil and the dialectic with the client and the latter usually makes the former possible. Once this painful decision was taken by client and architect, the task appeared clearer.

2. To design a building within a building, the inner with an organic plan responding to the necessities of use and the outer with a formal rectangular plan and volume responding to the scale of the adjoining building group. The intermediate space between the inner and outer envelope serves for climatic protection, assists the change of scale between the new and the old buildings, and is a psychological, aesthetic response to the client's wish to have an "open" house by replacing the usual exterior barrier wall and symbolic front door with a sheltered space that is both inside and outside.

3. To use a frame structure in order to free the inner enclosing skin and interior compartmentation on the three floors from load-bearing structural considerations.

On a minor decorative key there was a consistent preoccupation to create the union between materials of equal or different kind by covering or displacement.

11.5  View from the SW showing both the rural environment with the Montseny massif behind, and the proximity of the original summer residence built at the turn of the century.

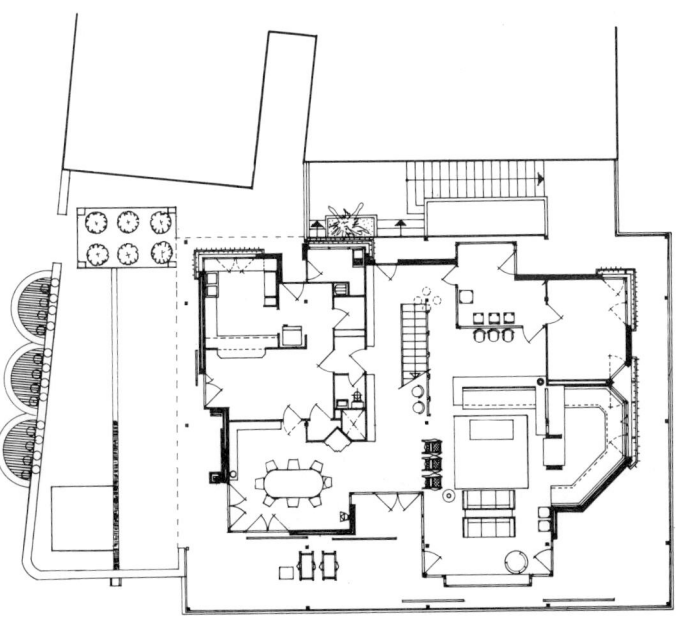

11.3  Plan Scale 1:300

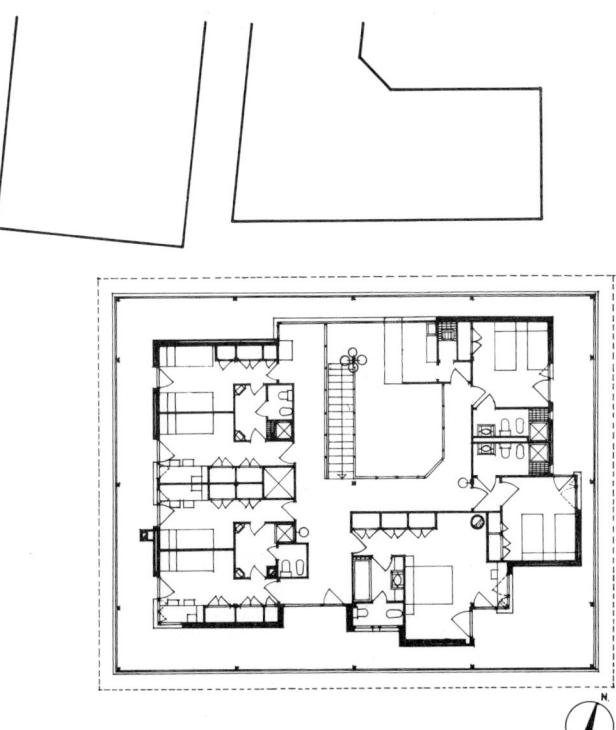

11.4  Plan Scale 1:300

11.6 The veranda. Note the detailing of the steelwork with the use of short cut-off common U-sections that supports the twin beam structure, and lower down, supports the structure of the balustrade. This ad-hoc detailing exploits the rudimentary technology of the artisan.

11.7 The living room looking towards the formal dining area. The intrusion of the terrace breaks up the interior space besides providing an exterior sheltered recess from the wind. The small glass panes are introduced where there are no supplementary blinds to protect the house from intruders when empty.

11.8    The E façade. The entrance is on the right under the veranda between the new and old buildings. The
veranda railing is formed by pre-cast concrete posts that accomplish the same function as the classical
stone balustrade of solid-transparency that combines privacy with visibility from within.

11.9    The living-area looking towards the entrance lobby (glazed screen) beyond the double-height volume of
the "hall".

# 12 CASA CASTANERA Es. Golfet. Calella de Palafrugell. Province of Gerona
1966
ARCHITECT: Antoni Bonet
CLIENT: Doctor, wife, and seven children (3 daughters, 4 sons)

SITE
3.000 m² (3590 yd²) on a steep pinewood slope between the
main road and the sea to the S of the bay of Calella.

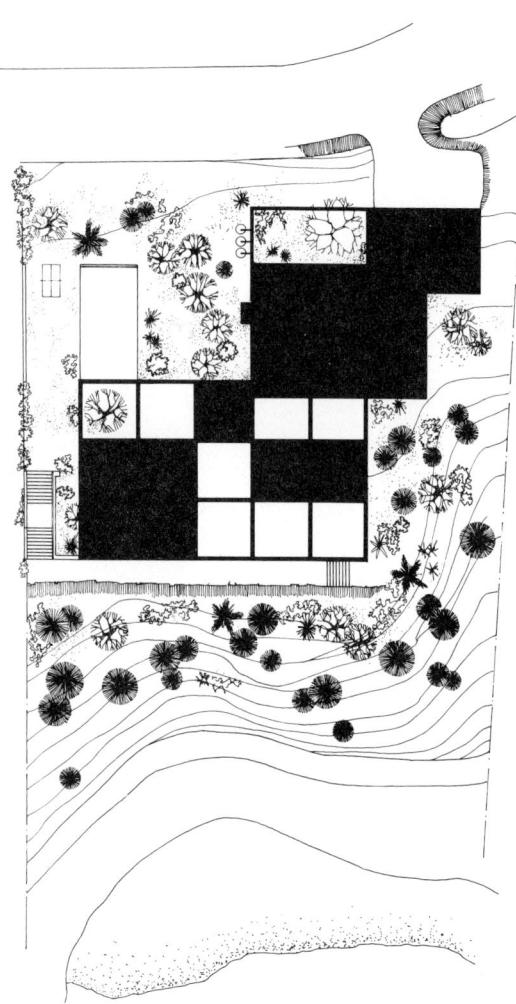

12.1   Site plan, Scale 1:670

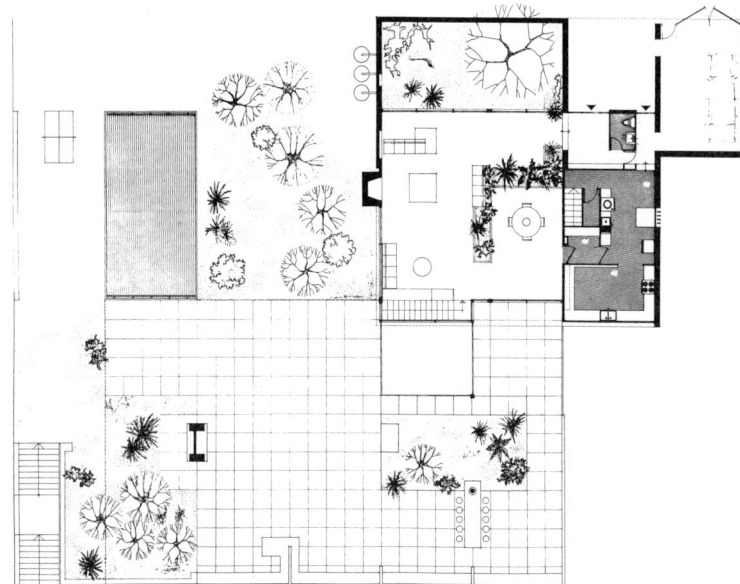

12.2   Plan, Scale 1:400

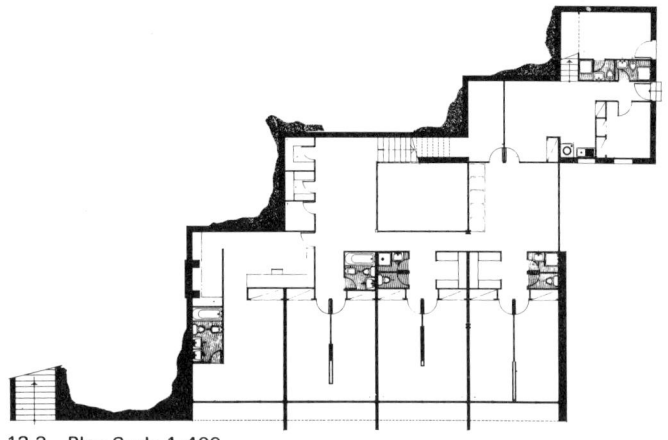

12.3   Plan Scale 1:400

PLAN
The house is carefully situated on the slope of the site in such
a way that the sea views and privacy of the bedrooms and
children's playroom is maintained by placing them below the
inside-outside living area platform.

The principal element of this platform is the immense porch
with its 25 x 15m (82 x 50ft) check-board awning 4m (13ft)
above it, creating pools of sunshine and shade through its open
and closed elements.

Behind this Mediterranean balcony is a 10 x 10m (33 x 33ft)
inside living room, with a dining area screened by plants. Cut

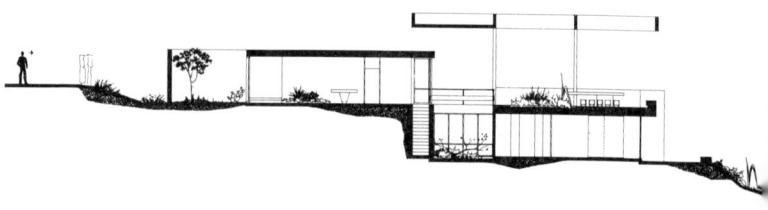

12.4   Section Scale 1:400

12.5   The largest room in the house is outside. The main support of the concrete sunporch is a combined barbecu, bar, and telephone booth. The sea is to the left.
The chimney-bar is an incongruous element that fails to resolve the bridge in scale between the
spectacular urban sunporch overhead and the domestic instrument itself.
The mixed use of steel and concrete columns contributes to this uncertain design. Note the other
architectonic furniture.

off on one side and adjoining the entrance is the kitchen and
garage with the servants' rooms below. These in turn connect
with the bedrooms through a multi-use ironing and sewing
room.

A sunken court, with a pebble and water pool floor, captures
the afternoon sun and lights the back of the lower bedroom
unit, and at the same time acts as a centre of gravity around
which the internal circulation of the house revolves.

## CONSTRUCTION
Reinforced concrete two-way span slab roofs and floors sup-
ported by steel columns in a 5m (16ft) grid, whitewashed walls
and varnished woodwork.

## OBSERVATIONS
Antoni Bonet occupies that rare position in modern architecture
of concurrently belonging to two generations. Like his fellow
countryman J.L. Sert, revolution and war snatched him from
the cradle of Le Corbusier's workshop in Paris to leave him in

cultural isolation in South America. Twenty years later he
returned to join the postwar generation. The result is that his
architecture has not lost the freshness of the schematic geometry of the first International Style. In the Castanera house
we find many of the characteristics of the Style as defined by
Hitchcock and Johnson. Its control of volumes, in this case
regularly growing along a diagonal axis, as can be clearly seen in
the site plan, and the concern for the intrinsic elegance of
materials—glass, concrete, steel and whitewashed solid walls.
Above all is the concept of volume as an open box, helping to
confirm the authentic claim of the building's intention to be a
representative example of modern architecture. The agile change
of scale from one element to another imposes an overall sense
of ordered architectural dominance tending to make the created
environment monumental, rather than human. Checking the
relations and filters of the topological distribution of the different parts of the house against Chermayeff's and Alexander's
community and privacy list, the positive result should be a new

architecture of humanism, but it is not. This indicates that
Chermayeff and Alexander had insufficiently developed their
thesis and that humanism needs other ingredients. Why is it
that the works of Antoni Bonet, Marcel Breuer and, to a lesser
extent, Josep Lluis Sert, that are otherwise so architecturally
correct, lack that poignant discord essential to a soul architecture alive to a moving culture. There is neither the pessimism
of Marcuse, nor the humour of Lewis Carroll, to disturb their
too tranquil interpretation of the modern movement.

12.6   A closer view of the relationship between the porch and the simple volume that encloses
the rest of the living area. The well of the court lights the bedroom unit underneath.
The contrasting scale between the two elements is well handled by visually lightening the
porch in opening half of its panels and supporting it all on thin steel columns, and by
fusing the small details of the enclosed living area in an overall repetitive screen of wooden
shutters. The open railing around the well seems inconsistent with the otherwise complete
separation of this reserved lower area from the rest of the house, and one feels that an
opportunity was missed to exploit this hesitant inconsistency by actually providing an
external staircase, or on the contrary, to enclose it even more.

12.7   The patio that lights the rear of the bedroom unit acts at the same time as a centre
of gravity round which the internal circulation of the house revolves.

12.8 View from the garden showing the interior living unit on the left and the porch over the Mediterranean balcony beyond. A small swimming-pool is on the right and the projecting "beams" on the left contain the shower sockets with the control taps sunk into the wall below them.

12.9 The inside living room looking towards the porch. The white wall that appears to be a cill wall is actually a balcony over the staircase to the bedroom area below. The dining area is on the extreme left. The floor to ceiling window, and door divisions, and low ceiling succeed in creating a relatively intimate atmosphere in spite of the size of the room. The formal L-shaped provision of indoor plants on the left (see plan) as a permanent division of compartments for defined activities introduces a scale and treatment usually reserved to public institutional foyers and adds an unsympathetic note to the space.

# 13 CASA DAHL El Castell, Lloret de Mar, Province of Gerona
1966
ARCHITECT: Josep Bonet (Studio PER)
CLIENT: A Shipping agent and wife with a married son with
children, and one unmarried son.

## SITE
1.000 m² (1200 yd²) lot in a more or less uncontrolled estate
development but with excellent views to the S and SW. The
site is level but 1.50m (5ft) higher than the access road.

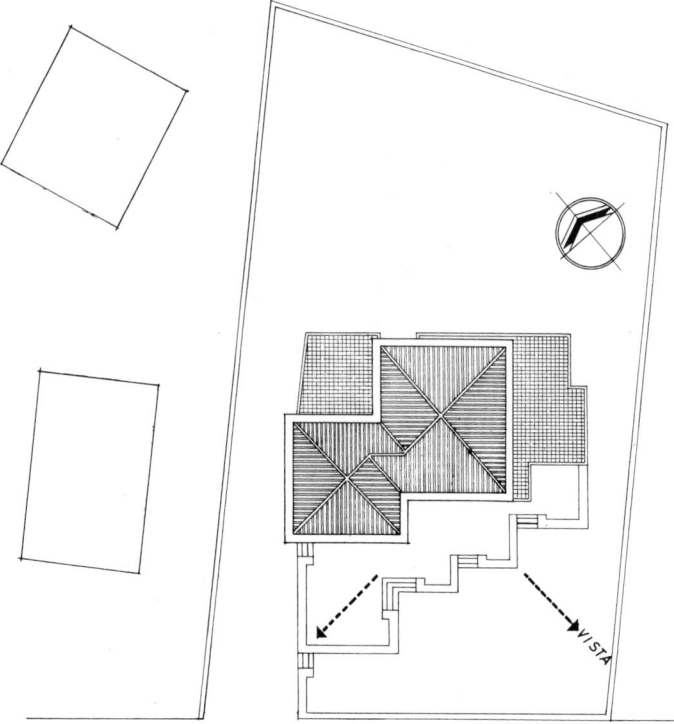

13.1 Site Plan Scale 1: 430

## PLAN
Essentially, two square enclosures, more clearly drawn on the
upper floor plan and roof, joined by the staircase. The ground
floor enclosure spreads out below forming extensive terraces to
the upper floor.

The ground floor itself is further extended into the garden
through the medium of staggered walled terraces between the
house and road.

The distribution of the rooms is unusual in providing a certain
independence for the three 'units', parents, married son, and
bachelor son. This independence suggested the provision of
segregated outside spaces provided by the first floor terraces.

The fashionable insistence of destroying the corners and edges
of intersecting planes has led to the repetition of corner windows
and balconies and the return of the colour-wash as a frieze under
the eaves and balconies. It has also led to a deliberate complication of the original form. Good views, only to the S and W,
diagonally to the orthographic direction of the house, functionally justify the corner windows.

## CONSTRUCTION
Load-bearing walls, tiled roof.

## OBSERVATIONS
The deliberate use of broken surfaces and volumes crept into
fashion during the 'fifties and 'sixties both because of the
desire to express a new-realism, (J.M. Richards' functionalism
of the particular, and a revolution of the casual picturesque
spatial possibilities of the urban setting, as found,) and the
desire to break away from the almost classical rigours of the
triumphal beaux-arts of Le Corbusier and Mies van der Rohe
and their minor fellow travellers.

This resulted in a chunky "new brutalist" architecture, but
brutal only because it broke with the accepted canons. It was
an architecture influenced by criticism rather than, as Gregotti
has pointed out, a commitment to architecture. The Casa Dahl
is a good example of this transitional style of architecture.

Moving from the general, where the positive interest in this
building lies, to the particular, the ambiguous entrance, and the
confused way in which the extended volume of the ground
floor is attached to the original double cubes weaken the
control over the composition considerably. The result,
especially to the back facade is very unhappy.

72

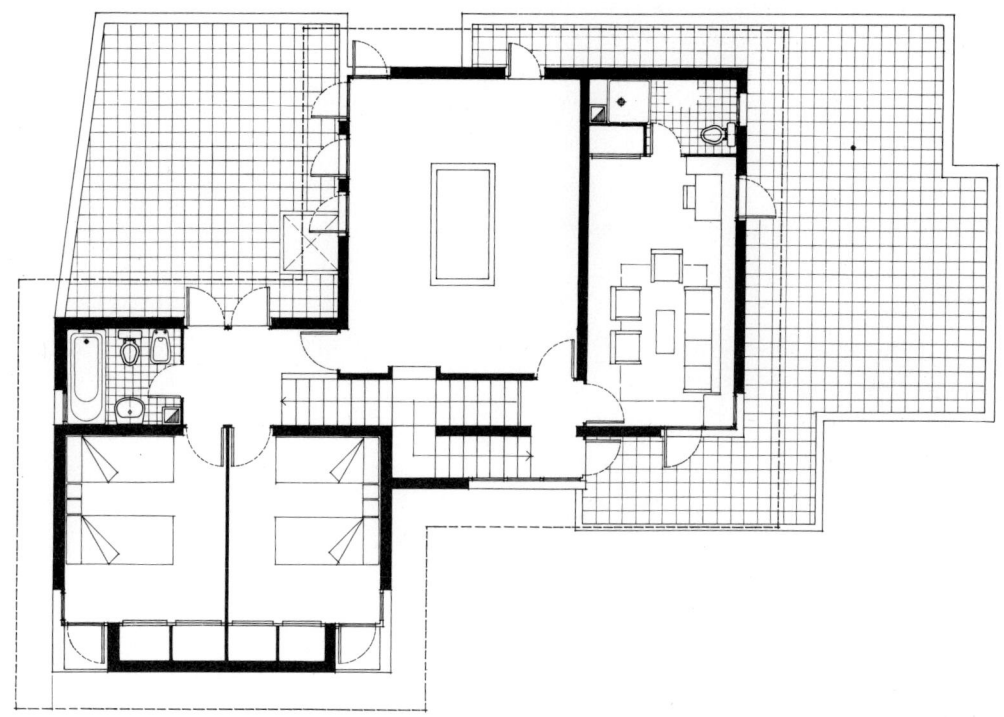

First Floor            13.2    Plan Scale 1: 130

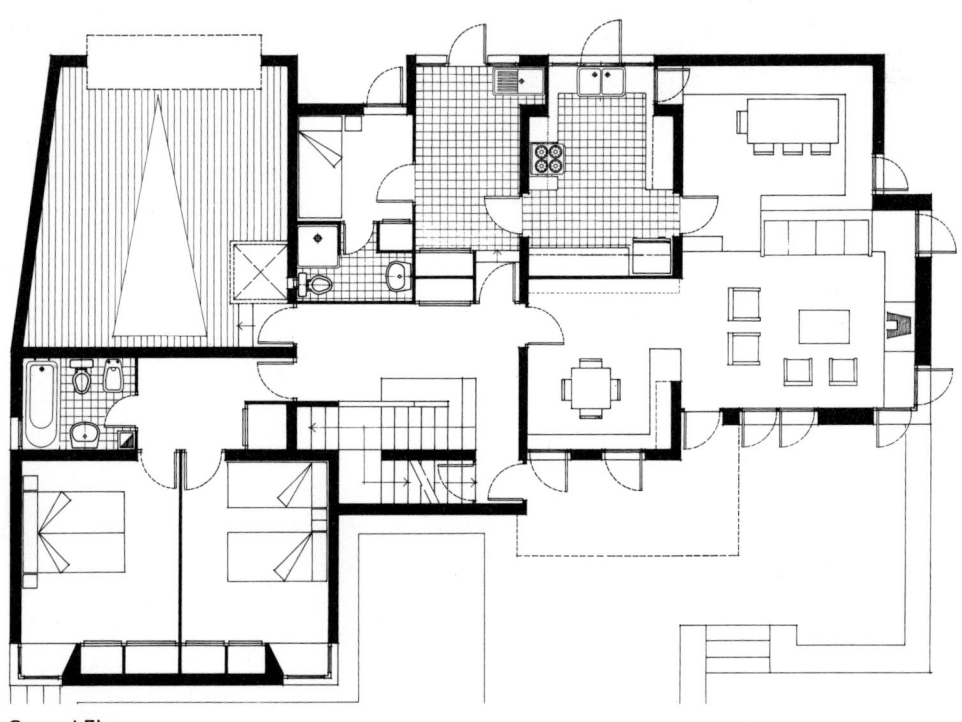

Ground Floor

13.3 The context of the 'estate environment' is not encouraging, and the critical experimental style adopted by the architect is a reasonable solution.

13.4 View from the W showing the 'front' facade. The bedrooms are in the foreground on the left and the living area is behind on the right. Note how the corner windows are recessed further back on the first floor to provide a small balcony.

13.5 View from the SE with the living area to the right foreground. The almost obsessive destruction of the corners and edges of the intersecting vertical planes is clearly evident. However the intersection of the eaves with the wall is left as a sharp pronouncement.

13.6 The rear facade. If the kitchen had not been extended out beyond the primary cube the result would have been less confusing, both on plan and in elevation. The garage door is out of scale with the rest of the building and has been left as such.

13.7 The living-room. The photograph is taken from the library and games' area looking towards the sitting area with the dining behind at a slightly higher level.

# 14  CASA IMANOLENA Motrico. Province of Guipuzcoa
### 1966
ARCHITECT:  Luis Peña
CLIENT:  Businessman, wife and their ten children

## SITE
2.000 m² (2392 yd²) halfway up a pine covered hillside looking N across the sea to France. Rainy climate.

## PLAN
A rectangular plan, with a pitched roof and peripheral porch
for climatic protection, gives a simple but ample volumetrically
compact mass in keeping with the isolated vernacular architecture of the Basque country.

The rooms are distributed around an interior court clad with a
pronounced, glazed triangular prism that admits sun into the
living area which faces N across the sea.

The house is entered by stairs from the garage below which
leads to a small compartment within, but open to the interior
court. From this, two doors lead into the entrance hall and
service rooms respectively.

The bedrooms and surrounding porch are on one level, with
the court, living, and service room level about 700mm (27in)
below.

## CONSTRUCTION
A structural grid of steel columns and trusses supporting a
double pitched tile roof that returns at porch height against
brick gable walls.

## OBSERVATIONS
The geographical, cultural, and political characteristics of the
Basque country provide a sharp challenge to any architect
working within the framework of the modern movement. Without sacrificing the objectives of formal, social and technological
investigation on the broad cultural front that knows no
frontiers, the architect must identify his work with whatever
tense local forces he encounters at that moment, and at that
place, by either absorption or opposition. To ignore these
forces would run the risk of an abstract or eclectic statement.
It is within these terms that one can write of the politics of
architecture.

The architect Luis Peña is never afraid to commit his architecture to the realities of this double role of the mature modern
movement. The *Casa Imanolena* is an excellent example.
Simple, massively built objects are part of the Basque vernacular architecture and harmonize with the landscape of the
valleys to become an accepted part of it. This does not contra-
dict the tendency of the modern movement's return to the
functionalism of the whole, often expressed in mega-structures,
into which the functionalism of the particular is fitted. The
peripteral arrangement of the structural columns of *Casa
Imanolena* creates a strong visual scale related to the whole,
rather than to the distribution of the domestic planning
arrangements within the building. However this mega-structure
has not been allowed to dominate the building in the trium-
phant way that Palladio did, rather it has been appropriately
tamed by drastically reducing the height of the porch and sink-
ing the living-room below the exterior pavement. Thus a real

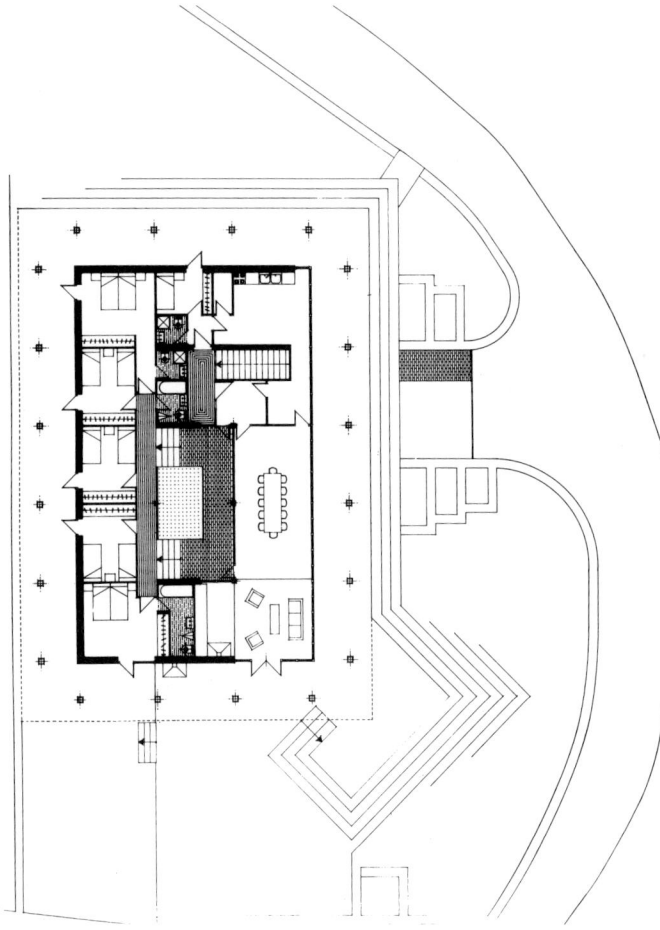

14.1  Site plans Scale 1:400        ➤ N

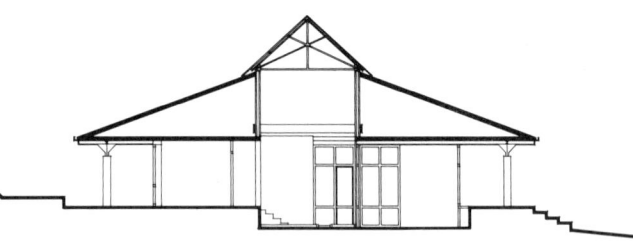

14.2  Section Scale 1:300

14.3　View from the S showing the dominating part played by the roof in the composition of the building.

protective feeling against the inclemency of the weather has been achieved, with the eye level of seated persons situated just above the floor level of the pavement of the porch.

The interior glass covered court creates a pleasant transparency besides acting as a catchment area to all the internal communications, however, the excessive height, detailing of the elements, and confused space over the entrance, add up to a cold and disappointing climax after the polished performance achieved by the building's external appearance.

14.4　View from the N showing the relative scale of the house to the landscape. The glazed wall that sweeps along and in front of the sitting and dining areas and kitchen is perhaps a little too schematic but is coherent with the idea of letting the whole dominate the particular.

14.5　The interior garden court giving access to the bedrooms. The rather harsh detailing and 'left-over' gallery is inconsistent with the exterior design.

14.6 View from the W. The low porch helps the house to sit snugly into the hill side and the slight complication of the roof and skylight add an essential note of interest.

14.7 The living area floor is below the level of the porch giving a greatly enhanced feeling of security from the rigours of a wet climate.

14.8 The N façade with the car porch and entrance below. The relation of this porch to the house is awkward as there is not sufficient separation to allow the position of the colonnade to be ignored.

# 15 CASA HUARTE Puerta de Hierro. Madrid
## 1966
**ARCHITECTS:** Ramon Vazquez Molezun, José Antonio
                Corrales
**CLIENT:** Construction industrialist and family

## SITE
A corner site of 2.000 m² (½ acre) in a garden suburb to the
N of Madrid.

## PLAN
A grid plan formed both by living areas and earth banks enclosing three courts. The first court serves the main living and dining rooms (the latter sunk below the floor of the court) and is
bordered to the E and S by large stepped terraces that protect
it from the roads. The dining room is connected to the main
living area by a passage that can be opened on both sides to
link the second court with the first. This second court contains
a swimming pool and sun terrace and is enclosed by a multi-
purpose room to the N that links the bedrooms with the main
reception area. Part of the room, which is split into two levels,
is used as a playroom for the children, otherwise it is really
just a wide passage to the bedroom wing that closes off the W
side of the second court. To the south, and under the planted
terraces, are the service rooms containing kitchen, laundry,
bedrooms and servants' dining room, together with a laundry
court and service entrance court. The third court is exclusively
bounded by bedrooms and high stepped terrace walling, within
which is a secluded sunbathing court.

Underneath the house is a ring of service galleries.

## CONSTRUCTION
Mixed steel frame and load-bearing brick structure, with tiled
roofs.

## OBSERVATIONS
The whole site, in this garden suburb of Madrid, has been
designed to maintain the privacy of the users, both inside and
outside the building, cutting off all visual communication from
the neighbourhood. It is in effect a keep within a castle of
concentric defensive walls. The analogy explains the form of
the house: the three courts, one for formal external family-
social relations by the living and dining areas, another for informal external-internal social relations, with a swimming pool
and terrace, by the games room, and finally the intimate bedroom court with a secluded sunbathing alcove, these are the
keeps of the castle; the puffed up, tiled, roofed grid flanks
these keeps in defensive positions which are further protected
by stepped, concentric, walled, shrubbed terraces that both
absorb the dungeons of the service rooms within its womb and,
like Birnam Wood, present an innocent foil to the street. But
this Dunsinane castle has its watch tower too with the dining
room roof springing up over the entrance to house a high library with a gallery to a look-out window over the falling
countryside beyond the immediate neighbours.

With the form thus forced into this unusual, defensive role, the
mellow style of traditional Danish, or Finnish brickwork, with
echoes of Aalto's Säynätsalo civic buildings, reminds one of
the eclectic role of Madrid architecture.

The total complement of interior and exterior spaces, the

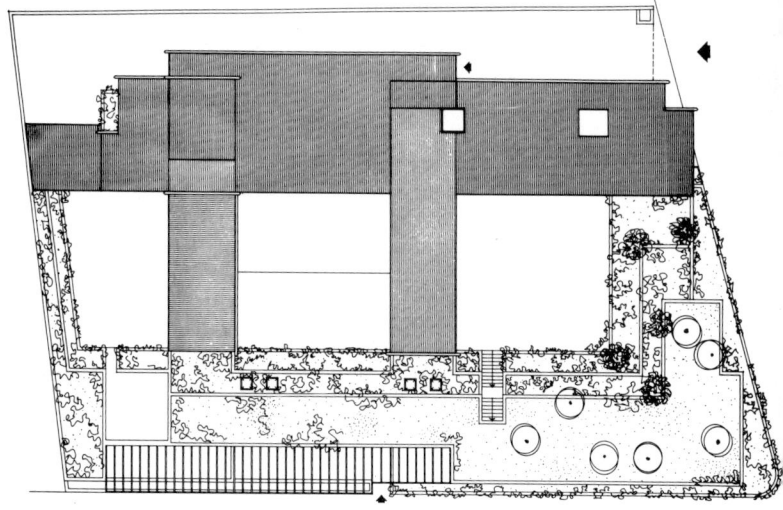

15.1   Site plan Scale 1:650

unity of material, the crisp edges of the planes that define the
form, the hierarchical social compartmentation of use, indicate
a strong architectonic control throughout the design faithful
to the reality of the building purpose: to create a domestic
citadel, within but apart from the garden suburb, that should
be seen to occupy the whole of the site clearly defining its
outer and inner social frontiers.

The question that this built-object begs is that however successful the aesthetic solution and no matter what dress the architect puts on it a building fails to arouse interest if it does not
touch the soul of architecture—where architecture in a state of
flux is involved both with formal investigation (establishing a
coherent language with its own symbol system) and social
commitment.

On the first count the formal investigation of the Casa Huarte
is limited to the subservient role of forcing the scattered volumes, and the treatment of each one, to relate to its purpose of
forming and protecting the inner courts. The parts are conditioned by the whole, which is the key to all good architecture,
but if the parts themselves suffer through the extreme applic-
ation of the law, as the schizophrenic treatment of served and
service volumes shows, then the interest in the formal result
wanes. In other words one suspects that the general formal result has been obtained by a trick. On the second count, the
social commitment of establishing a subtle relationship between privacy and community has been upset by designing a
typological inversion of garden suburb values of a community
living in a through-flowing park. This house has been built in

the wrong neighbourhood for the understandable privacy desired. A row of Dunsinane castles owing allegiance to a nirvana sub-culture of the elite is a frightening social prospect for the urban scene.

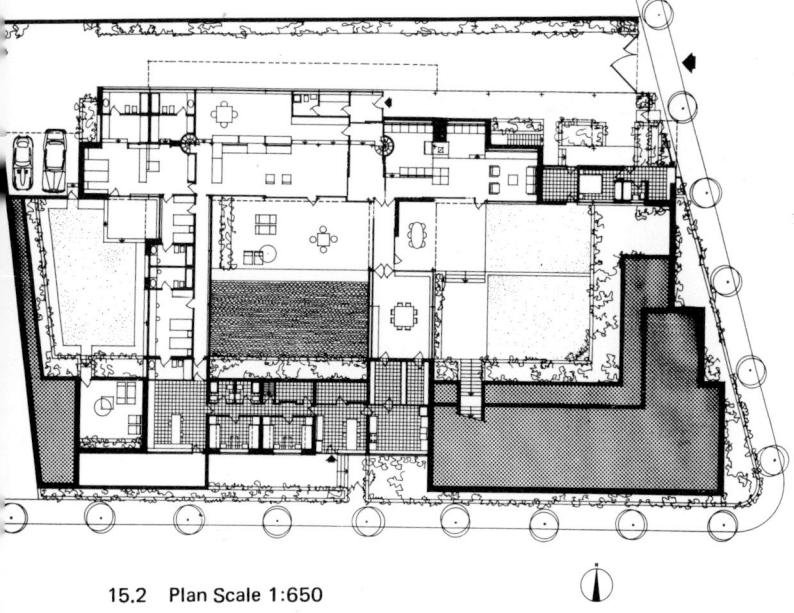

15.2 Plan Scale 1:650

15.3 View of the first, and main, court with the dining room and living room windows forming two sides overlooking the garden towards the stepped terraces from which the photograph is taken.
Note the artificial, high walls over the windows that have been designed to exclude views into the court from neighbouring houses. The volume that rises from over the dining room and reaches out over the living and entrance area contains the house's only lookout over the countryside.
*(Photographs 15.3-15.8 are reproduced by courtesy of Editorial Blume)*

15.4 The stepped and walled terraces protect the first court from the road to the E and S opposite the living and dining areas.

15.5 The second, and inner, court is in reality completely enclosed by the dwelling, but the effect is different since the service rooms are hidden beneath the stepped terraces of plants that run right across the site bordering the road. The careful detailing of the brickwork, the sharp edges of the arrises, helped by the metal gutter, show a mature architectural check over the otherwise disintegrated collection of volumes.

15.6 The entrance gate and porch. The glazed corner of the caretaker's room (just above and behind the number 1) successfully turns the corner of the entrance porch around and over the oblique boundary wall. The excessive empty roof volume above dangerously leads the building away from the rigours of architecture into the realm of sculpture.

15.7    The central fireplace in the main living room is superbly handled as an axis around which revolve various activities on different levels. In the foreground is a bar-trap table.

15.8    The outside dining porch within the angle between the dining room and living room in the first court.

# 16 CASA GOMEZ  Soto de la Moraleja. Alcobendas. Madrid
## 1967
ARCHITECT:  Rafael Moneo
CLIENT:  Business man, wife with three children

SITE
2.500 m² (2690 yd²) on one of the rises of the undulating
heaths of the plain around Madrid.

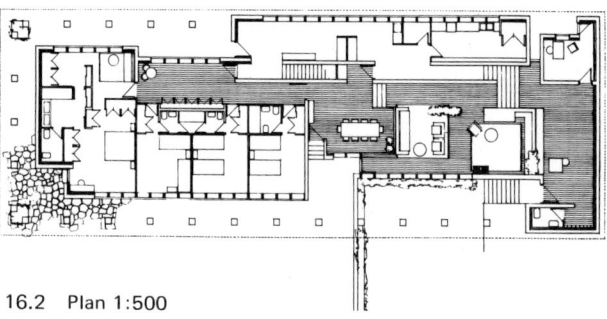

16.2   Plan 1:500

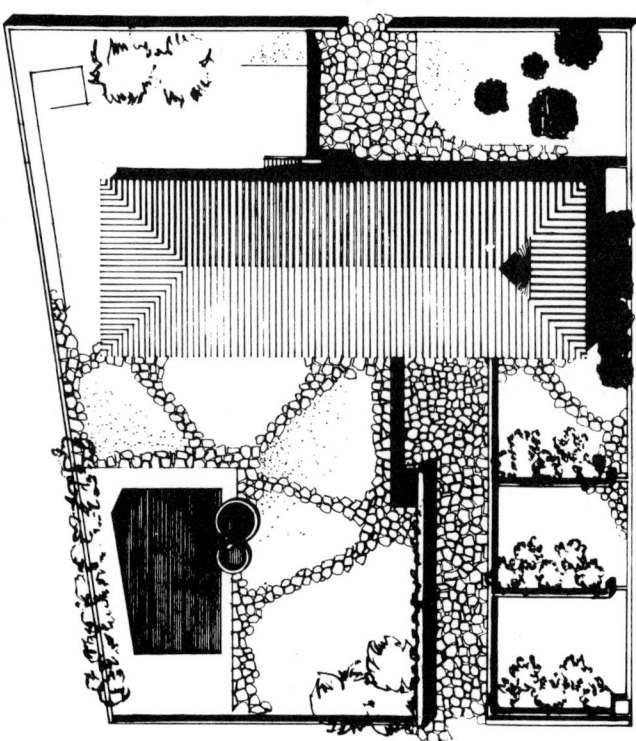

16.1   Site plan 1:600

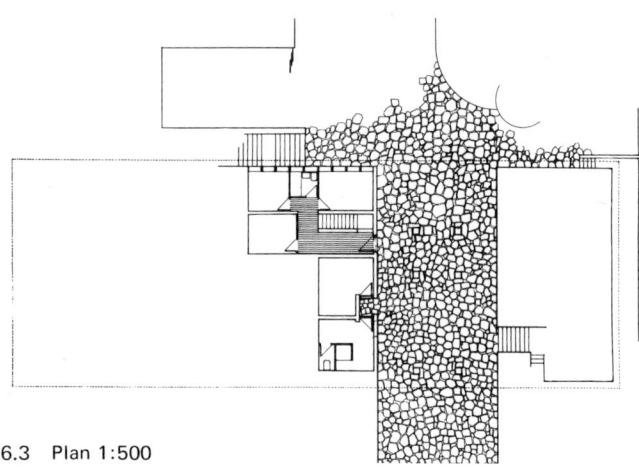

16.3   Plan 1:500

PLAN
The living area is a lined sequence of slightly enclosed compartments staggered off to one side of a rising processional
route, from the porch and entrance, where there is a small
hide-away study, ascending through the sitting and dining
spaces to the bedroom area.

The service area, with kitchen and laundry, lies parallel to the
processional route to its N with a series of connections at each
level. A secondary staircase which serves as a short cut to the
bedroom area leads from the porch into the laundry.

The self-contained bedrooms, for guests, children, and parents,
are grouped around two sides of a vestibule that with its low
ceiling and generous width becomes in effect a spacious secondary living area for more domestic use.

A deep porch protects the W and S walls from the sun.

The house is penetrated perpendicularly to the main axis by a
sunken, vehicular access, forming an entrance porch below the
principal floor. Adjacent to the porch are the servants' sleeping
quarters.

CONSTRUCTION
Load-bearing brick walls and pillars with concrete beams support a tiled roof.

OBSERVATIONS
Is Rafael Moneo's *Casa Gomez* a Madrid version of Frank
Lloyd Wright's Prairie house? A Madrid Usonian? Natural
materials, the open plan, the ribbon window, low slung roof
plane, built-in plant boxes, movement round a central fireplace,
narrow modulated fenestration, and even a car porch that goes
through under the house serve as a visual reminder of Wright's
Herbert Jacobs House (1948) which provides the vocabulary

16.4 View from the S showing the sunken vehicular approach on the right that leads to the porch that penetrates the hill under the house. Above it is the living area and to the left the bedrooms. The stately rhythm of the colonnaded porch gives a quiet order to the variation of ribbon windows and wall planes: this concentration of interest, or 'decoration', contrasts with the blank end wall to the E.

common both to Wright's houses and to Moneo's *Casa Gomez.* Whereas Wright's houses grew out organically into the natural surroundings by extending the walls, balconies and roof planes successively beyond the generative interior functions, Moneo restricts this growth to a simple controlled volumetric unity. A Latin, if not pure Mediterranean, cultural discipline has imposed its own version on the basic model. The lesson to be drawn is there. Applying the reasoning of Bevan, and Domenech, one can note that the *Casa Gomez* is a case of naturalizing, or assimilating and synthesizing a foreign influence but, as Chueca points out, that goes on everywhere all the time. What is new about this Madrid Usonian is its casual compartmentation articulated within an open plan, its volumetric simplicity, and its concentrated areas of 'decorative' contrast between the colonnaded porch and the almost bare blank walls of the rest that together contain the built volume itself. The idea of revolving

*movement* around the chimney is another enrichment of a basic theme of Wright's. On a different scale, one is reminded of the approach from behind to the Parthenon itself in the way Moneo has arranged his processional route into the living area from the porch, always turning until one faces the opposite direction.

16.5 View from the N looking towards the punctuated wall containing the study window and light shaft to the turn of the entrance hall inside.

The agreeable vertical proportions of the punctuation and windows balance the otherwise monotonous horizontality of the volume: it also indicates the double height of the entrance hall and study. The light shaft also coincides neatly with the change of direction of the concrete beams supporting the return pitch over the E façade.

16.6 The double height porch of the entrance with the living room windows to the left.

16.7 The living area looking towards the dining compartment with the porch through the strip windows on the left and the door to the reserved bedroom area on the right. All the exterior woodwork is painted a lacquer red.

16.8 The chimney centrepiece around which the 'processional' entrance revolves from behind and below then up on the left along the wall. Natural light is introduced from above to highlight the spine wall.
Note the lower ceiling over the entrance hall corresponding to the turn of the pitched roof over the E wall.

16.9 View from the N through the entrance porch. The service area is above with the servants' sleeping quarters below to the right.
—Barely visible in the photograph is a shadow line, caused by the advance of a panel of brickwork, running over the porch and continuing on the left. The way this panel is drawn is purely arbitrary and has been designed for aesthetic effect. This anarchic breaking of the canon of logical, justified decoration, so close to the heart of the modern movement, is strong and worrying. The danger of frivolity is somewhat confirmed by Moneo's repeated use of this effect with rather dull results in other buildings by him in and around Tudela.

G

## 17  CASA BELDA  Rambla del Jardin 83. Valldoreix. S. Cugat del Vallés. Barcelona
1968
ARCHITECT:  Miguel Alvarez
CLIENT:  Speculative house for Summer letting to a large family

### SITE
700 m² (840 yd²) narrow, rectangular lot cut back on a 3m (10ft) flange building line. The neighbourhood is a nondescript suburb relieved by pine-covered low hills.

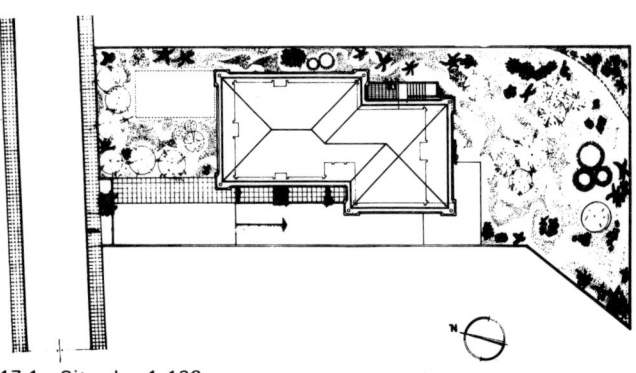

17.1  Site plan 1:166

Nevertheless the *Casa Belda* is a skilled example of opium architecture. The drug is stimulating, with shots apparently directly administered by the Master: window-lintel frieze dividing the wall planes into upper and lower sections with different finishes, from the Winslow house; broad overhanging eaves, corner boxes and plant boxes, from the Martin house; extended garden walls with strong protecting skirting and coping, from the Robie house. The Wright drug of course has had its earlier addicts from the Dutch (House at Huister Heide by Rob Van't Hoff, for example), followed by others, which makes it respectable drug-taking.

### PLAN
A hybrid composition between two engaged rectangular enclosures, as expressed by the pitched roof, and like Frank Lloyd Wright's Unity church an articulated plan-diagram with the entrance between the day and night wings. The slope of the site is exploited to accommodate a garage under the day unit at the back of the house. The early style of Frank Lloyd Wright's Prairie houses is reinterpreted without inhibitions, forcing a certain formality of a symmetrical arrangement of the elements, of which the built plant box plays a conspicuous part.

The two rectangular enclosures are staggered to admit the run-up entrance on one side, and the steps down to the garden on the other.

### CONSTRUCTION
Load-bearing brick walls, tiled roof.

### OBSERVATIONS
The architect Miguel Alvarez has rightly pointed out the difficulty he has met designing several houses for the *bourgeois* overloaded with demanding and pretentious conditions for ostentatious social display. He has met this in the only way possible by introducing an alien formal order. This can be given its run for a time but ultimately the desire for an aesthetic based on the reality of the problems involved must reject this opium of an alien formal order in exchange for a proper architectonic dialectic.

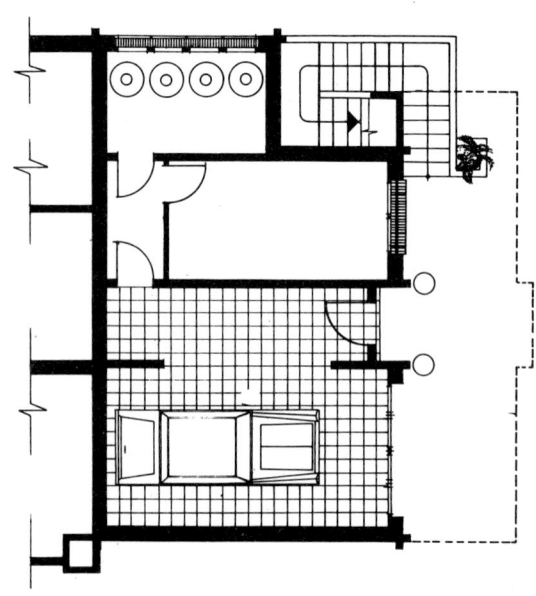

17.3 The entrance. The bedroom unit is to the left with the living unit projecting out to close off the entrance which is between the two. The ramp leads down to the garage at the back. Note the play of textured surfaces between the major and minor elements. The formal veneer of each plane is emphasised by strong corner pilastres that contain it.

The string course that runs along at lintel level is introduced so that the rendered surface above can be painted the same colour as the ribbon that runs along the edges of the soffit of the eaves in order to destroy the sharp internal arris between the two planes, — a sensitive corner detail that is successfully played up to become a major element in the design.

17.4 The W façade showing the living unit with its deep projecting balcony terrace. The gutters broaden out at the angles to avoid swirl over the vertical "gargoyle" spouts, and, of course, to repeat the corner profile of the brick wall below.

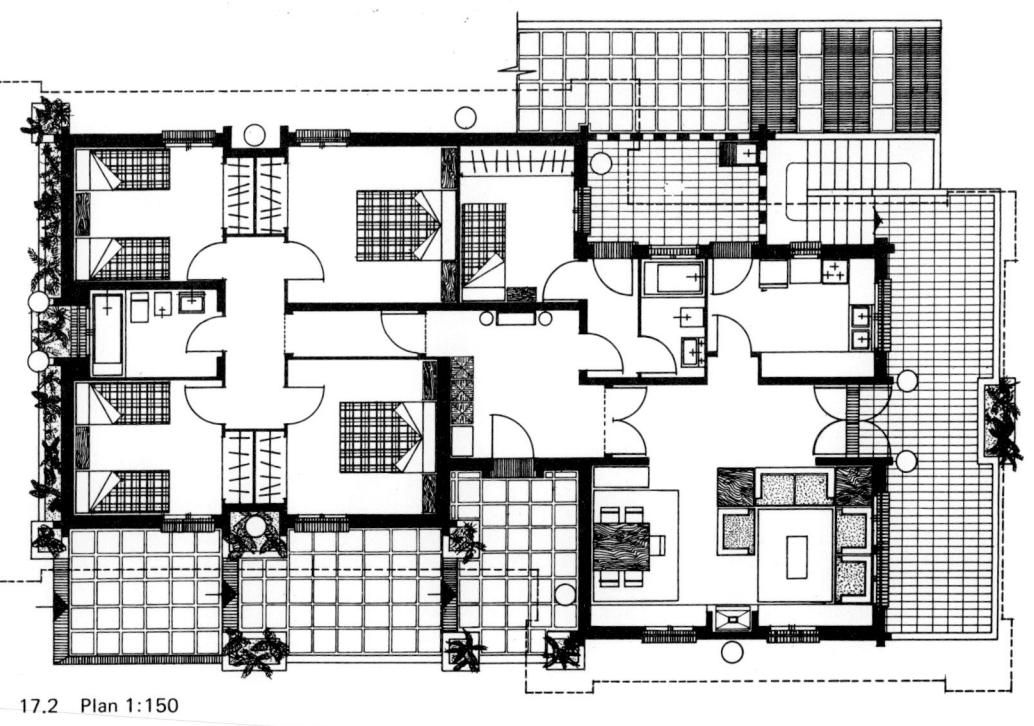

17.2 Plan 1:150

17.5 The N and road façade. The rich, formal treatment of this blind wall is no less real because it responds to an idea of the function of the whole in its environment, rather than a response to the functions of the particular.

17.6 The S façade. The living area is above with garage and utility room below. The symmetrical emphasis is maintained to impose its extra-architectural order despite the displaced balcony terrace which is skilfully handled. A sudden economic cut by the client caused the omission of the original design plan of completing the walls with the same treatment as the other three façades.

## 18 CASA CRUYLLES Aigua Blava. Palafrugell, Province of Gerona

1968
ARCHITECT: Antoni Bonet
CLIENT: Lawyer and politician, with four children (1 girl,
3 boys)

### SITE
9.300 m² (2¼ acre) in a pinewood valley, between the main
road above and the sea below, in the bay of Aigua Blava.

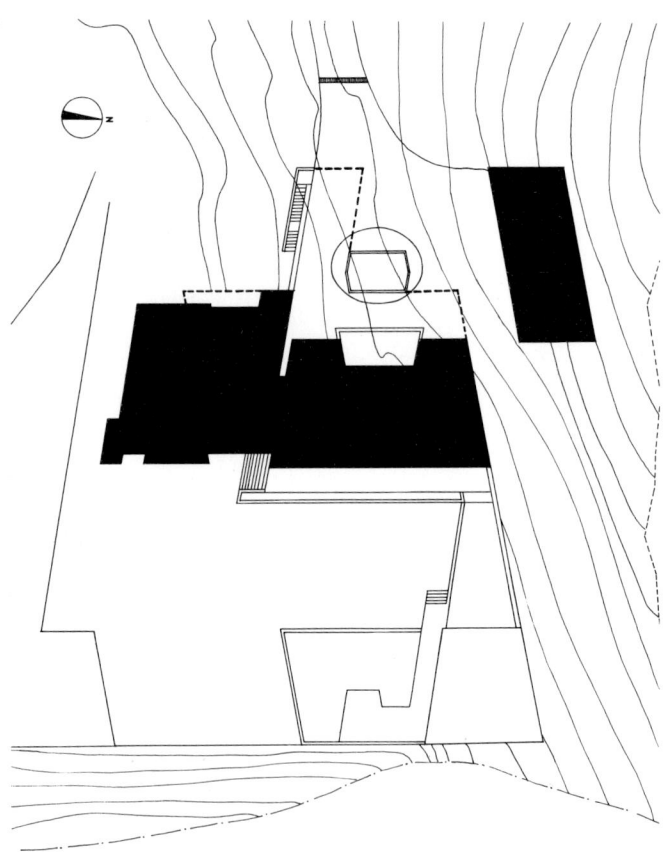

18.1   Site plan 1:600

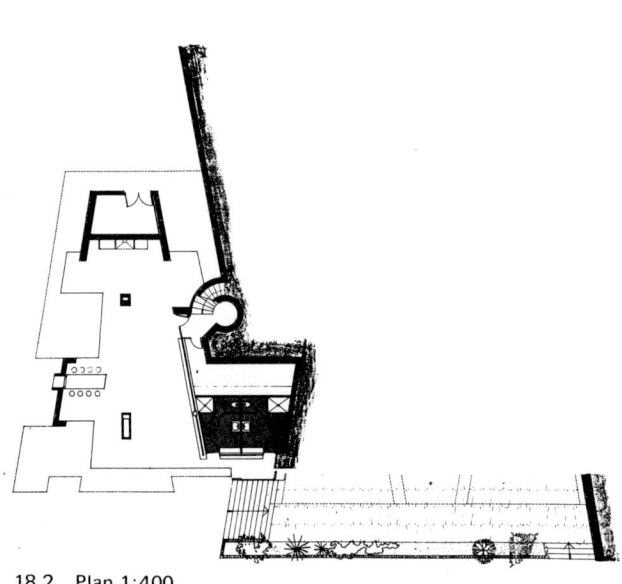

18.2   Plan 1:400

### PLAN
The slight opening out of the valley as it touches the shore is
echoed in the trapezoidal plan adopted by the architect. The
steep slope of the site with the approach from the access road
above led to the placing of the garage and entrance at the roof
level.

To give more weight to the entrance, two guest rooms sharing
a trapezoidal plan are situated behind it, independent from the
rest of the house. The vaulting of the main living area below, a
flotsam of traditional Mediterranean architecture, is inverted
over these guest rooms to accentuate and give interest to the
entrance.

A wide spiral staircase connects the entrance to the split-level
floor below. An L-shaped group of bedrooms, including a
study that overlooks the rest of the living area, wraps around
the S and E (seaward) sides of the staircase. The living area is
attached to the lower arm of the L and is vaulted with three

interlocked trapezoidal vaults that project out to form a porch.
Behind and parallel to the living area are the kitchens and service quarters, below ground level.

Below the bedrooms, and half a floor height below the living
room, is an agreeable left-over space that serves as shaded outside dining and sitting area.

### CONSTRUCTION
Load-bearing walls, concrete slabs and vaults.

### OBSERVATIONS
Sert's Maeght Foundation in Saint-Paul-de-Vence and his
earlier studio for Miró in Majorca are immediately recalled on
seeing Bonet's *Casa Cruylles*. The interior is reminiscent of
Yamasaki and Edward Stone. All, in one way or another, are
trying to evolve the International Style without letting go
it's rudimentary creed. The results of their desire for enrichment and complication of form, without losing the clarity of

the movement's elementary geometrical schemes, make it doubtful if it is really possible to achieve their aim. This entertaining play of form risks being superficial and is opposed to the reality of architecture's cultural role of interpretation and provocation. Nevertheless the recourse to alien poetry (where the work is given an energy beyond its capacity) can result in successful pictorial composition. However, the mere involvement with form in this abstract way serves to remind those who prefer to wrest form from the hard reality of the situation that besides a committed architecture there also exists an alternative way of formal investigation. While the handling of

scale throughout the whole of this very large house is very successful, through the strength and repetition of the forms adopted, the trapezoidal plan and vaulted section, the correspondence between function and form is ambiguous in the various treatment of the bedrooms. The inverted vault and solid wall below it on the main E façade seem to express a monumental activity that, in reality, does not, and cannot occur. The union between this volume and the vaulted living area, with its split level differences, is a difficult and awkward formal problem that has not been successfully solved in the composition of the main façade.

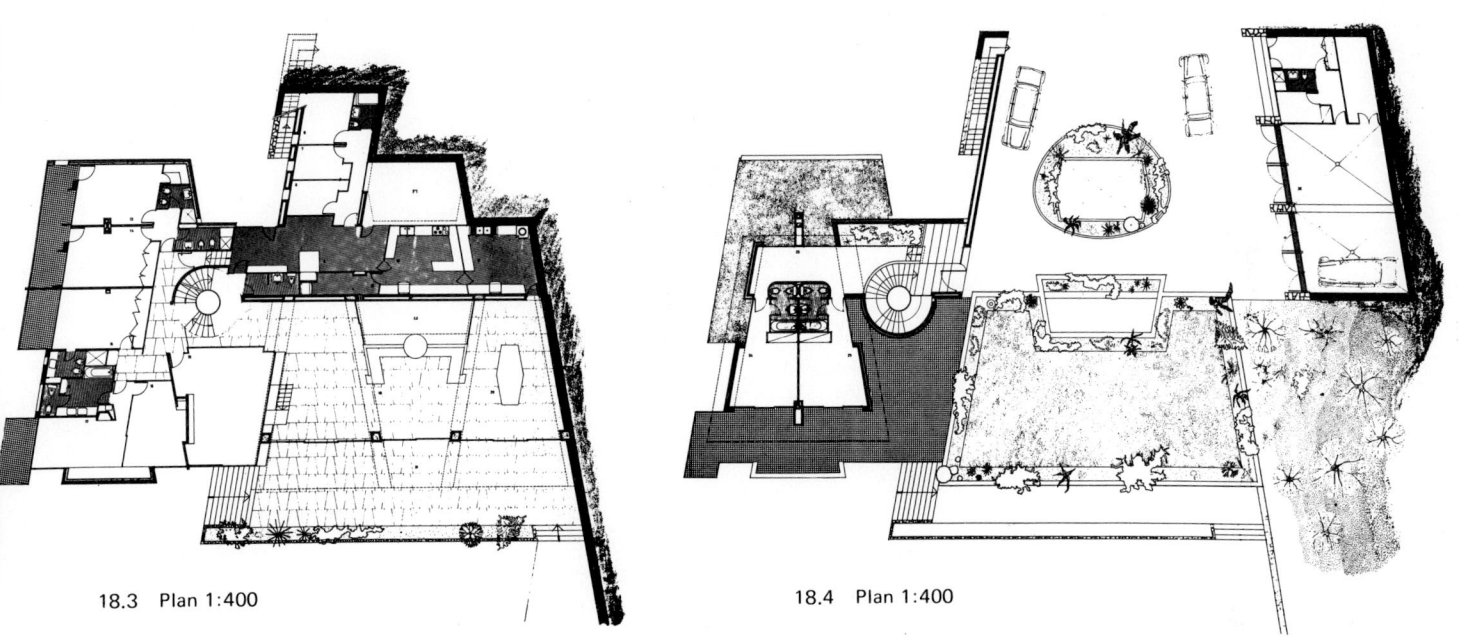

18.3   Plan 1:400

18.4   Plan 1:400

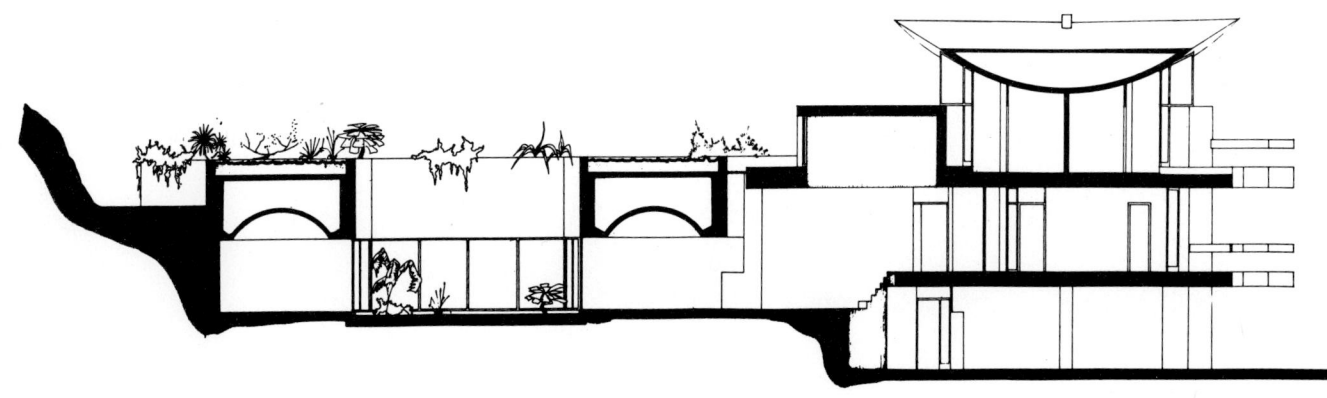

18.5   Section Scale 1: 225

18.6　View of the E façade of the house from the shore. The contrast between the vertical accent of the bedroom group and the horizontal accent of the living area reads well as a basic composition. This is further underlined by inverting the vault over the bedrooms. Given the scale of the building, this play of form to give an architectural unity to the whole is legitimate, but dangerous as it relies on the anarchy of alien poetry rather than on the systematic vocabulary of reality.

18.7 The S façade. A view of the children's bedrooms with the vaulted guest rooms above, and dining porch below. The rather odd introduction of stone intrudes a little surprisingly upon the otherwise disciplined use of limited materials. The contradiction between the deep protection from the sun given to the children's bedrooms, and the naked exposure of the guests', underlines the danger of free poetry.

18.8 The E façade: The bedrooms are to the left with the living area to the right. The formal difficulty of joining the vaulted volume to the rest of the house can be clearly appreciated.

18.9 View from the study through the glass screen and non-structural decorative arches to the living area. The interior patio behind the hooded fireplace admits the afternoon sun that brings a transparent liveliness to the whole interior.

18.10 A view of the study from the living area. The spiral staircase can be seen on the extreme right. Note the absence of fussy details and unity of colour in order to express the simplicity and dominance of the enclosing form, even though in itself it tends towards a decorative complication.

## 19  CASA HEREDERO  Tredós. Vall d'Aran. Province of Lérida
1968
ARCHITECTS:   Josep M. Martorell, Oriol Bohigas, David Mackay
CLIENT:   Industrialist, wife and five children (boys and girls,
ages 4—18)

### SITE
4.500 m² (1 acre) isolated at an altitude of 1.200m, just below
the *La Baqueira* ski runs and overlooking the small village of
Tredós, 5 hours by car from Barcelona. Steep NE—SW slope.

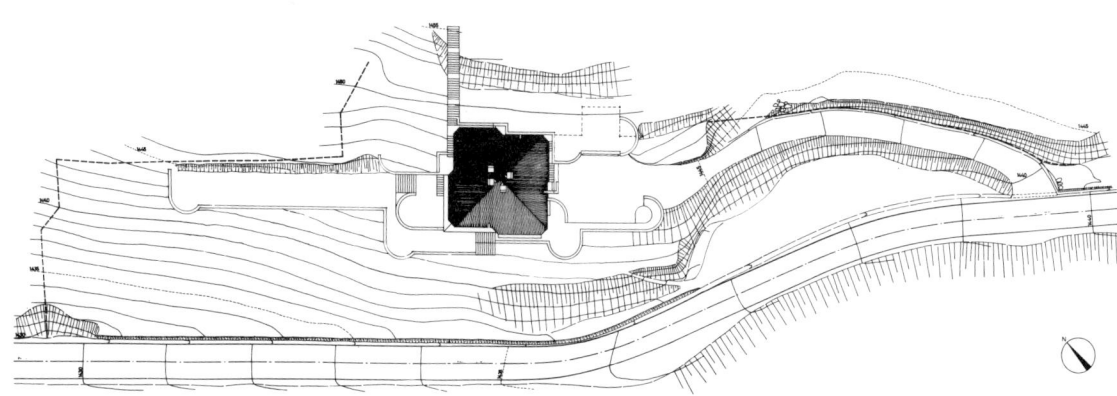

19.1   Site plan 1:1200

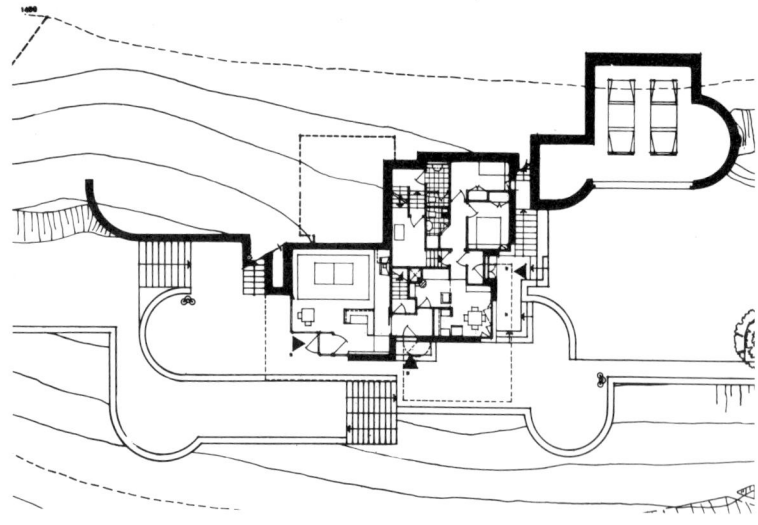

19.2   Plan Scale 1:500

### PLAN
A compact cluster of four internal compartments around a
central chimney-services-staircase core. These four compartments, with independent structure and services, in staggered
relationship with one another through accented 'bridges', and
capable of growing out independently on a diagonal axis, are
given a visible image externally by the descending roof ridges,
and internally by the diagonal-boarded ceiling. The four compartments are repeated on each floor, always with the chimney
and services concentrated at the angle of the central core,

which become, in effect, the elements that generate the geometry of the design. On the ground floor, one of the compartments is replaced by the mountain itself owing to the slope of
the site, while two are occupied by the caretaker's flat, and the
fourth forms the entrance for skis, and those coming in from
the mountain, when space is needed for changing and keeping
the equipment. This compartment serves also as a 'dirty' living-
room with a large open fire for indoor barbecues. On the principal floor one compartment is taken up by the laundry, kit-

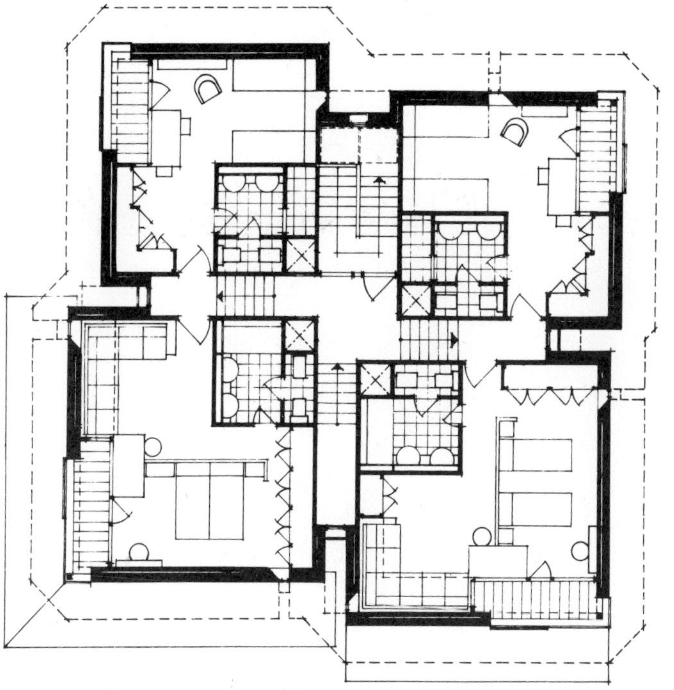

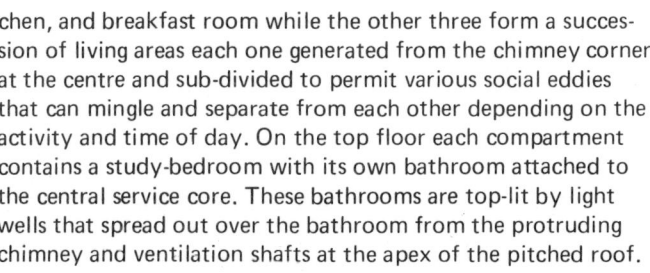

19.3 Plan Scale 1:200

19.4 Plan Scale 1:200

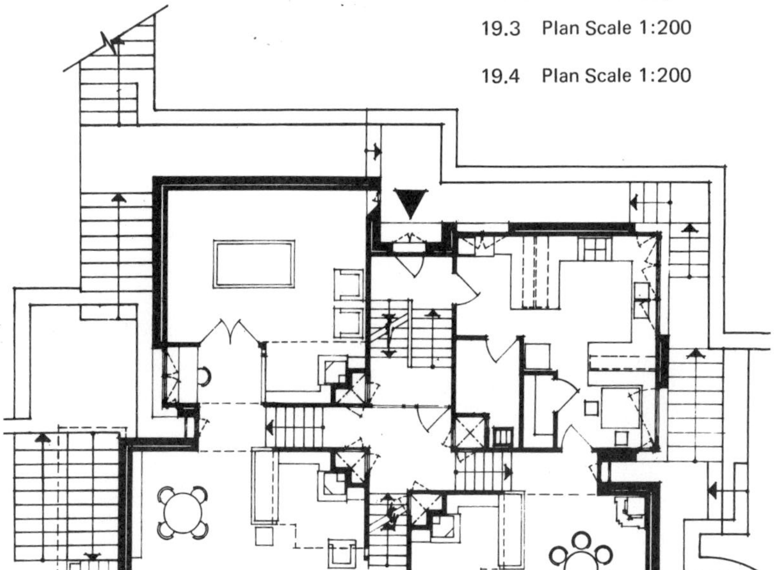

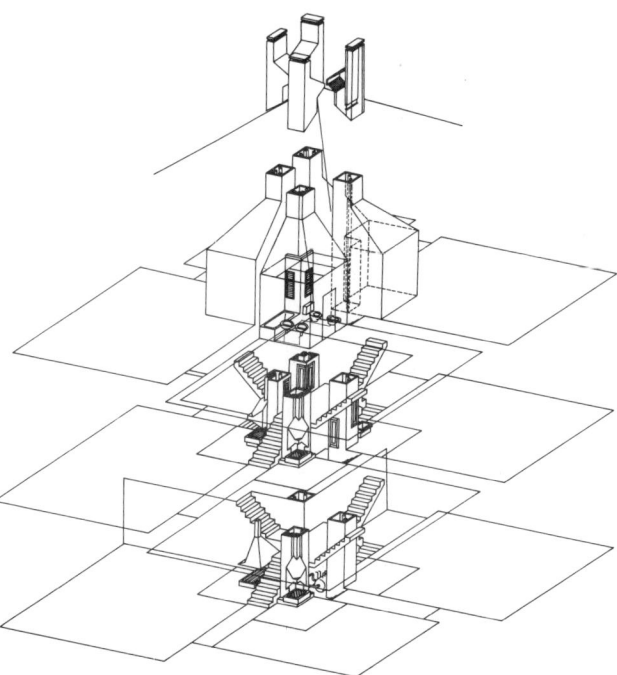

19.5 Detail of the central chimney-services-circulation core showing the broken cruciform staircase between the four service shafts.

chen, and breakfast room while the other three form a succession of living areas each one generated from the chimney corner at the centre and sub-divided to permit various social eddies that can mingle and separate from each other depending on the activity and time of day. On the top floor each compartment contains a study-bedroom with its own bathroom attached to the central service core. These bathrooms are top-lit by light wells that spread out over the bathroom from the protruding chimney and ventilation shafts at the apex of the pitched roof.

The basic element of the central core is the broken cruciform staircase with a common half-landing at the centre between the four service shafts. The stair flights divide the four compartments and articulate the space between them and the other floors in such a way that the rigid concept of a stairwell is dissolved into a gentle successive movement up or down through the interpenetrated compartments. Each arm of the stair flights cuts the corresponding façade with a tall window so that each compartment is 'readable' from the outside although each one is covered by the same pitched roof whose apex generates the pitches from the axis of the central core.

CONSTRUCTION

A steel frame supports floors and slate roof, and the enclosing double walls are of insulated and rendered blocks. The house was erected and ready for occupation in eight months between the snow seasons.

19.6   The W corner of the house. The large windows and balcony of the principal floor command a dominating view of the whole valley to the small town of Viella with the peak of Aneto beyond. The four central ducts contain, chimneys, service tubes, light and ventilation shafts to the core of the house. The height of these snorkles is designed to keep the inlets and outlets clear of the snow that might accumulate.

## OBSERVATIONS

*. . . . . . . . . . . . . . . . . . . . . . . . . . . . ." in an*
*up-thrust, crevasse-and-avalanche, troll country,*
*deadly to breathers,*
*. . . . . . . . . . . . . . . . . . below the melt-line,*
*where tarns lie frore under frowning cirques,*
*goat-bell, wind-breaker, fishing-rod, miner's*
*lamp country," . . . . . . . . . . .*

[*W. H. Auden "City without Walls"*]

These lines from the *River Profile* by W. H. Auden capture the fast silent dominating scale of this troll country just below the melt line. The environment of place was all pervading. But the answer was already there in the close compact village *objects* that dotted the valley almost touching each other. To merge with the mountain would have been out of character and a timid mistake, to cry out against it would have been bad manners. A fine, topological balance had to be aimed at. A regular complexity of a simple skin-tight volume, dark materials with a provocative reflective aluminium paint to slight the traditionalists, and long stone walls that stretch out under the house to meet the mountain, these are the main elements used to achieve this balance. Apart from the interest the house may have as a solution to the personal necessities of one family, which is of questionable interest if only the ethics of social value is considered, its value may lie with its attempt to extend the field of architectural investigation and experience beyond the client's immediate requirements.

One of these is the formal generative criterion described above which, within a coherent geometrical unity, permits the accommodation of the necessities of a complex program with the possibility of different volumes related to the whole and a certain degree of independent modelling and decorative treatment of each of its parts.

Another is the intention of creating an expressive fluid space, not only between the compartments on each floor, but in the connection between each floor by eliminating the continuous stair-well that would isolate the different floors. By forcing the circulation through the compartments on the principal floor the fourth dimension is not only acknowledged but exploited.

But perhaps the most fruitful and most difficult field of investigation is the suggested ambiguity of the built object in attempting to bridge the gap between the past traditional architecture of the valley and possible future solutions. With the exception of the slate roofing (imposed by the local bye-law aesthetic regulations) the materials used are foreign to the local tradition. However, the volume and tight surface treatment of the building attempts a recognizable dialogue with the adjoining villages. The steel structure, the solid planes of earth grey walls, and the galvanized iron railings, are the essential materials used to define these volumes that attempt a first step away from a 'folk-lore' mountain vocabulary to re-establish a real dialogue between architecture and place.

19.7 The SE and 'entrance' façade. The image of the compartment plan diagram is expressed in the vertical cuts that lead into the central core. The fascia is also slit to admit one narrow sky window to each bedroom which otherwise has only low lintel window balconies with restricted vertical views.

19.8 Skin surface with stretched laced "see-through stockings" over the windows is going towards a sensory aesthetic in architecture. Detail of the SE façade.

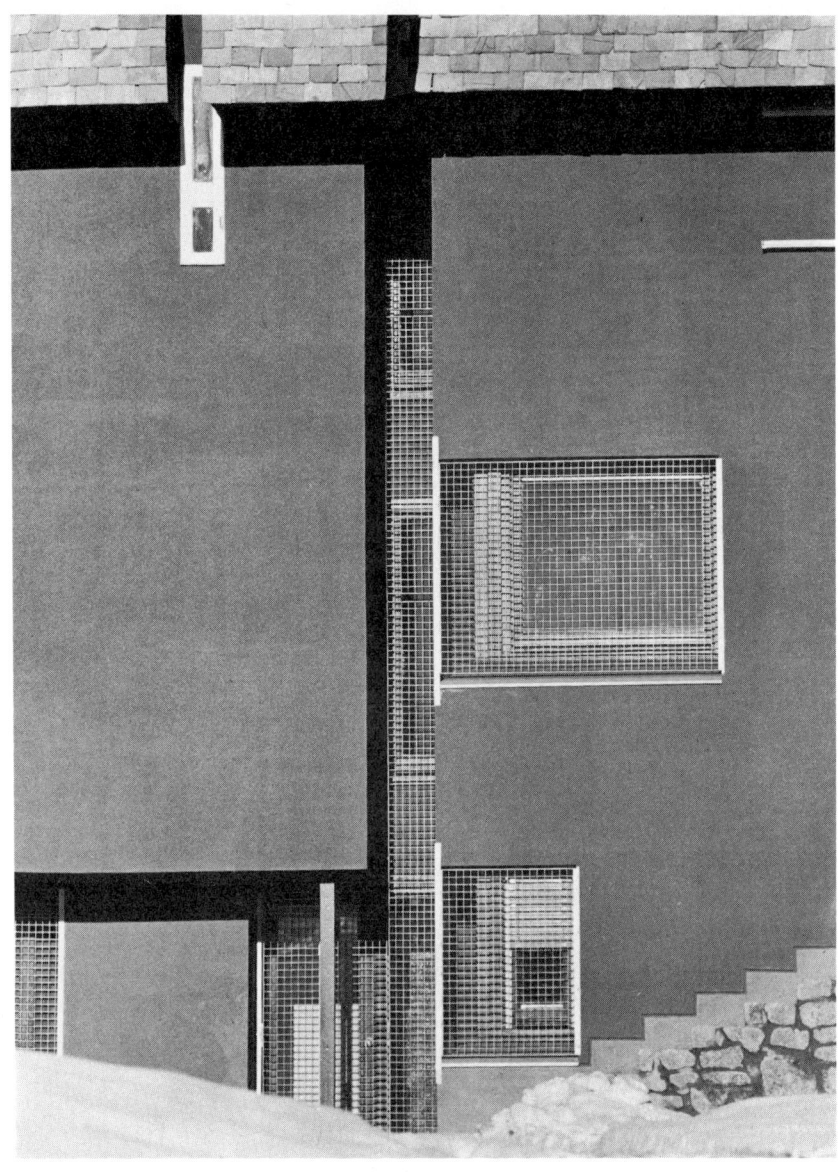

19.9 The kitchen is divided into three activity areas, cooking and washing-up, the laundry, and an informal dining or breakfast area.

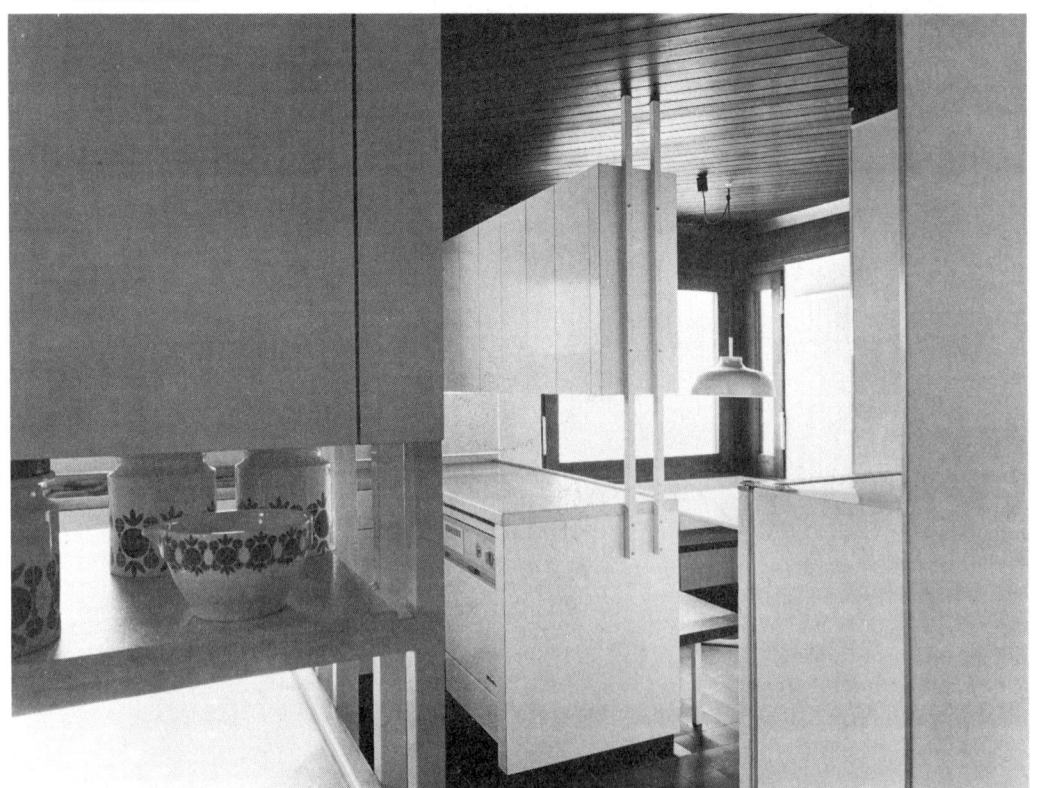

19.10 The fireplace corner of the dining area with the half-flight stairs up to the central landing on the left.

19.11 The living area from the dining space with the fireplace corner on the right backing into the service core. Note the diagonal ceiling boarding that expresses the direction of designed growth from the central core.

# 20 CASA URQUIA  Camino de Boixadors, main road Lérida to Huesca, Province of Lérida

CASA GARCIA
1969
ARCHITECTS:   Lluis Domènech, Ramon M. Puig, Laureano
                        Sabater
CLIENTS:   1. Lawyer, wife and five children (eldest aged 12,
                  3 girls and 2 boys)
              2. Business man, wife and 12 year-old son (2 married
                  daughters who might occasionally stay with them)

## SITE
4.500 m² (1 acre) in the fertile plain of Lérida, in a fashionable
residential area developing around the Tennis Club 2km (1¼
mile) along the main road to Huesca. The site is level but
borders a ravine to the North.

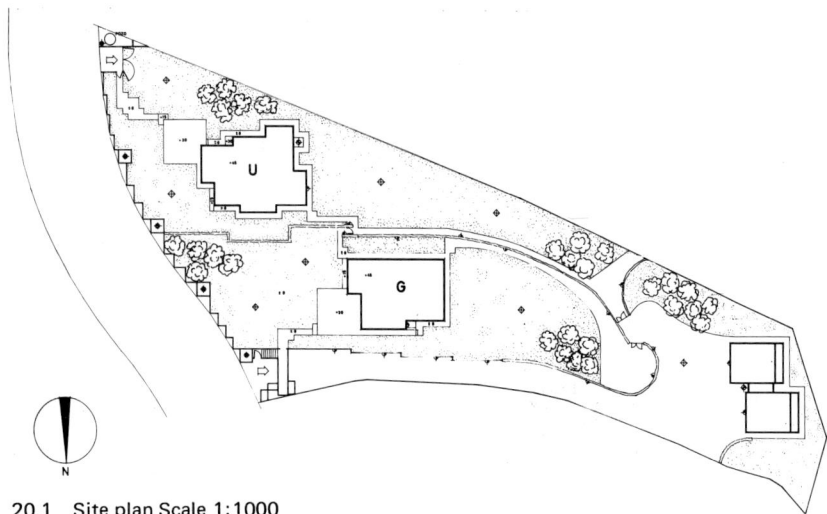

20.1   Site plan Scale 1:1000

## PLAN
Two separate but similar houses that almost share the same
site.

Each house has the same conventional planning arrangements
but with minor differences, consisting of an articulated living
and dining room that turns around the fireplace, with kitchen
and service on the ground floor, and bedrooms on the upper
floor.

A porters lodge and shared garage are at the end of the garden.

Neither house has a conventional entrance which has to be
effected by either passing through the kitchen or from the
porch directly into the living room (The houses were intended
for informal week-end and vacation use only).

The essential compositional elements used in the two houses
are: unity of materials, with brick walls, asbestos-cement roofing, blue metal chimneys and guttering; standard details like a
common window module, pre-cast stone cills and blind boxes,
etc.; a complex pitched roof that spreads down and out from a
single apex to finish with a wide eaves overhang. Finally to
introduce an accent on the differences between the two houses:
one has projecting balconies and the other has terraces incorporated below a lower pitched roof skirt that wraps itself
around half the house.

## CONSTRUCTION
Load-bearing brick walls, hollow tile floor slabs, and black
asbestos-cement tile roof.

## ARCHITECTS INTENTIONS
*"The original intention was that of implanting a program which
consisted of a compact construction aimed at increasing the
privacy and intimacy of each house by means of the proper
recourses of architecture (broken volumes, zonal interchanges,
etc.) and at the same time allotting maximum importance to
the garden, thus avoiding two long, strip lots. However this
was not accepted by the clients. Each insisted in having 'his
house' entirely different and isolated from the other and also
'his garden' with its distinct boundaries."*

*"As to the function of the house, any proposal which tended
to escape from the schematic conventionalism of the clients'
wishes, was likewise abandoned."*

*"The main interest of the restricted brief was the aim of an
architectonical environment that would function with the
traditional planning called for in the clients' program. The
difficulty was to stimulate the clients' sensibility just beyond
their expectations without shocking them into a refusal. (In
reality a 'little Swiss house' was the clients' image of the
project)."*

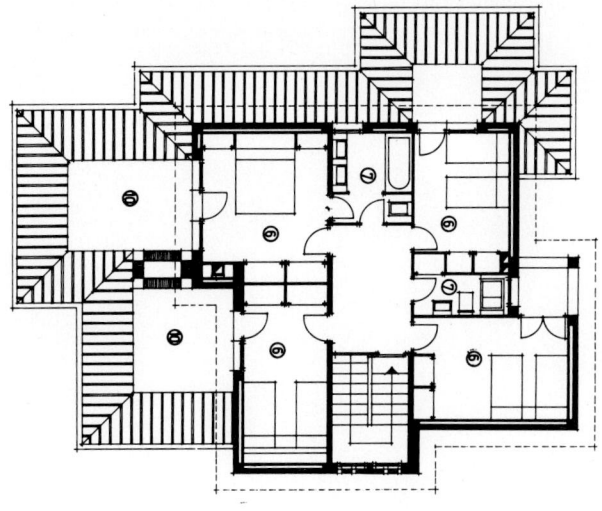

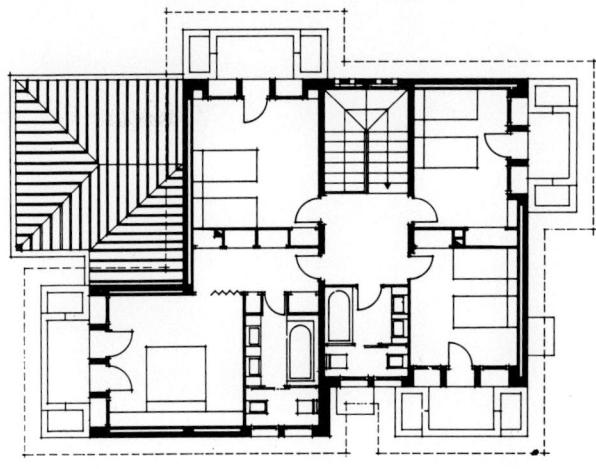

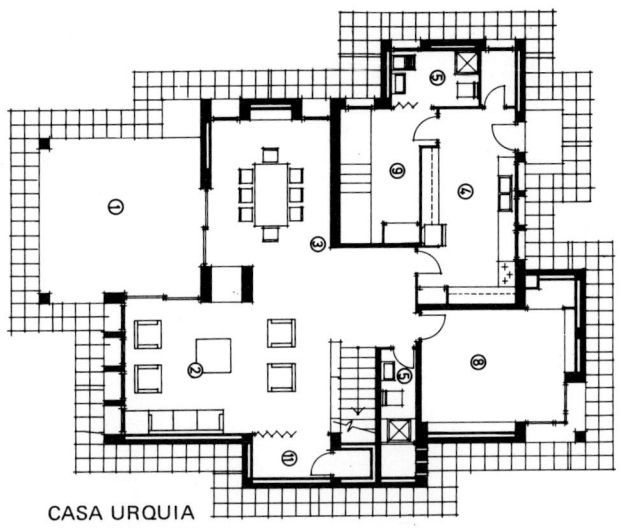

CASA URQUIA
20.2   Plan Scale 1:225

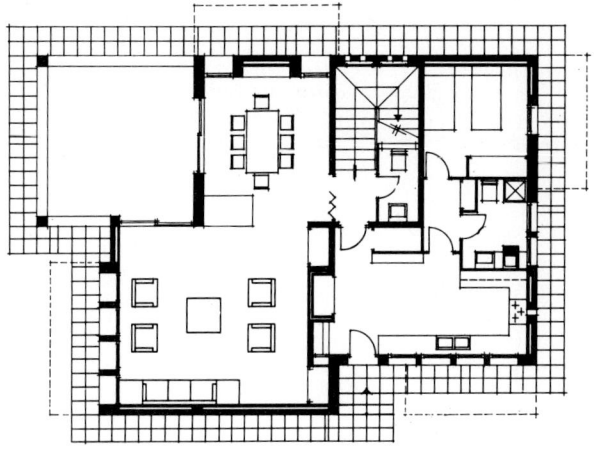

CASA GARCIA
20.3   Plan Scale 1:225

*"This intention has been maintained in what may be considered as 'construction.' Since a total control of the finished interior was difficult, a completely defined 'Architectural' packing was chosen."*

*On the other hand, the formal relationship among the various constructions of the 'complex' exists at a level of individual element design as well as at an 'image' level.*

*"A non-identical 'family of forms' is the result of individual differences in the design of some of the elements such as balconies, terraces, etc."*

*"Considering the impossibility of a control of the landscape-gardening an orderly structure was obtained in the exterior spaces by using a series of terraces and paths of rigid construction."*

## OBSERVATIONS

These two houses in Lérida are of exceptional interest more for what they are not than for what they are. The architects have not, as mentioned in the explanation of their intentions, tried to 'escape from the conventional institution.' In this they have not set out to break with the so-called traditional communicative architectural language as understood by their clients,

but have tried to force the signs of this language into an unusual relationship in order to awake a more sensitive awareness of the visual elements that make up living environment. In other words the authors have rejected organic architecture and pretended to follow the spirit of Howard Van Doren Shaw in apparently competently defending variations of the *status quo* rather than the innovations of Frank Lloyd Wright.

The Milanese look about these houses reminds one of Gregotti's early domestic work—and the whole Italian neo-realist movement and its opposite pole neo-liberty that both depended greatly on their superficial detailing, with historical-technical overtones. In a country where the social failure of society rarely produces the cultured client, attempts at soft didactic architecture are almost surely doomed to superficial understanding.

Although these houses have an agile poetic image, the lack of spatial relationship within the house and between the two houses leads one to conclude that the image has been applied externally as an alien agent only, rather like the icing of a plum cake. However what is interesting are the tactics used to weaken the very language used by the bourgeoisie and this fulfils a real but minor social role of architecture, and it is in this field that the buildings should be studied.

20.4 E and front façades of the two houses. On the left, *Casa Urquia,* on the right *Casa Garcia.*
In spite of the different compositions the resulting image is their similarity, which is given surprising force by the presence of the unified road wall. If this property limit had been non-architectonic the harmony between the two would have been seriously weakened.

20.5 View of *Casa Urquia* from the N with the entrance drive going off to the right. The orthographical relationship between this broken property wall following the rising curve of the road and the two houses has been firmly established, giving an ordered dignity to the urban composition.

20.6 SE view of *Casa Urquia.* The deceptively conventional language has been given a subversive twist by omitting the front door, using asbestos-cement on the roof, having only one window module, exposing the concrete foundations, separating the roller blinds from the window frame, and, above all, applying a style throughout the design that revalues traditional detailing.

20.7 The *Casa Urquia* incorporates the balconies within the volume.

106

20.8   The deep porch that forms a rational and coherent outside living space attached to, but separate from, the house and garden.

20.10   The soft, didactic architecture is pleasing in its honest constructive explanations. Alas, the consumer society is led by the blind, and many honest battles have to be lost before it can be expected to appreciate the subtleties of the aesthetic message.

20.9   The *Casa Garcia* projects the balconies beyond the volume.

107

## 21 CASA BRICALL c. Santa Coloma 98. Vilasar. Province of Barcelona
### 1969
ARCHITECT: Cristian Cirici (Studio PER)
CLIENT: Stockbroker and wife, with three married children,
two girls and one boy, who visit them

### SITE
400 m² (4300 ft²) rectangular plot behind a row of fishermen's
houses that form the sea front of the village. Apart from the
original buildings, the recent enthusiasm for summer houses by
the *petit bourgeôis* from Barcelona, echoing the low cultural
requirements of the European mass tourist invasion, has turned
this, and other coastal villages, into a tragi-comedy pastisse of
folkloric anarchy. The views, and "as found" environment, are
negative. The interpretation of local byelaws adjusted to
accommodate the speculation of land only encourages further
anarchy.

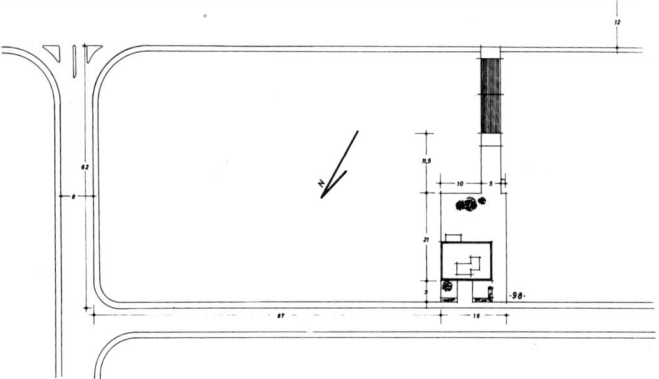

21.1 Site plan 1:2000

### PLAN
Two-storey rectangular building with a semi-basement accommodated under half of the split-level ground floor plan.

Volume of the house is kept to a simple cube with three
facades, the fourth being left as a party wall.

The distribution of the rooms is conventional with the exception of the staircase and complex spatial play of the living area.

As the main staircase rises through the house its volume is
incorporated into the adjoining space, first on one side through
a glass screen with the garage, then on the other, the entrance
hall, then again on the opposite side, the bedroom landing.

The living room is a cascade of increasing volume from the
dining area, by the games corner, to the main sitting area that
leads on to the garden court behind the house.

Immediately over the dining area is a secondary staircase that
gives access onto the roof terrace. The balance of volume under
the flights of this staircase has been incorporated into the
volume of the living area: two sides of its enclosing walls form
a translucent screen that admits light and partial views from
the bedroom landing and a small gallery.

### CONSTRUCTION
Load-bearing, rendered walls, hollow tile floor slabs, and a flat
roof.

### OBSERVATIONS
A recent visit by the architect to Vienna might cause speculation
that a revaluation of Adolf Loos was not absent when the house
was designed. The austere, puritanical, cubic design of the exterior volume, its tight enclosing skin (more akin to the 'twenties
than to Loos), its smooth interior detailing, and volumetric
play of space with the staircase, show an understanding of Loos'
contribution to architecture.

Another reason for the imposed discipline of the simple cubic
form was to punctuate the banal pop-culture of the hetero-
genous collection of neighbouring houses with a counter-point
of silence. Like the naked girl in a hippy community recalling
the origin of form and beauty of smooth young skin, this design
makes a subversive sweep of the decorative complexities of
fashion for its own sake. Complexity is not rejected but exploited in the varying volumes and controlled movement
through them of the living area. This is intended to compensate
for the spatial expansion usually enjoyed in the privacy of
garden living, here difficult to maintain when a tall block of
flats or hotel can be built next-door.

Within this context it is difficult to understand the handling of
the entrance into this complex living space. The entrance door
is empty of symbolic significance or preparation; it could lead
the unsuspecting to mistake it for a cupboard. This reminds
one of Saarinen's Dormitory buildings in Yale, or Rudolf's
architectural and design school in the same city, for the same
lack of cultural awareness of transition from one place to
another. It is a cheap way of achieving surprise.

Apart from this failing, the overall interest lies in the question
of fashioning the design in a reinterpretation of some of the
basic premises of the first International style, inherited from
Adolf Loos; architecture as volume as opposed to mass. It is a
swing away from what J.M. Richards once called "the functionalism of the particular" to the functionalism of the whole.

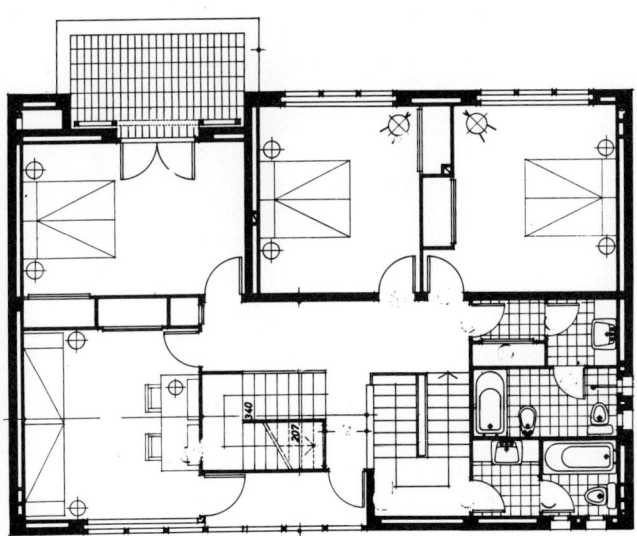

21.2    Plan Scale 1:600

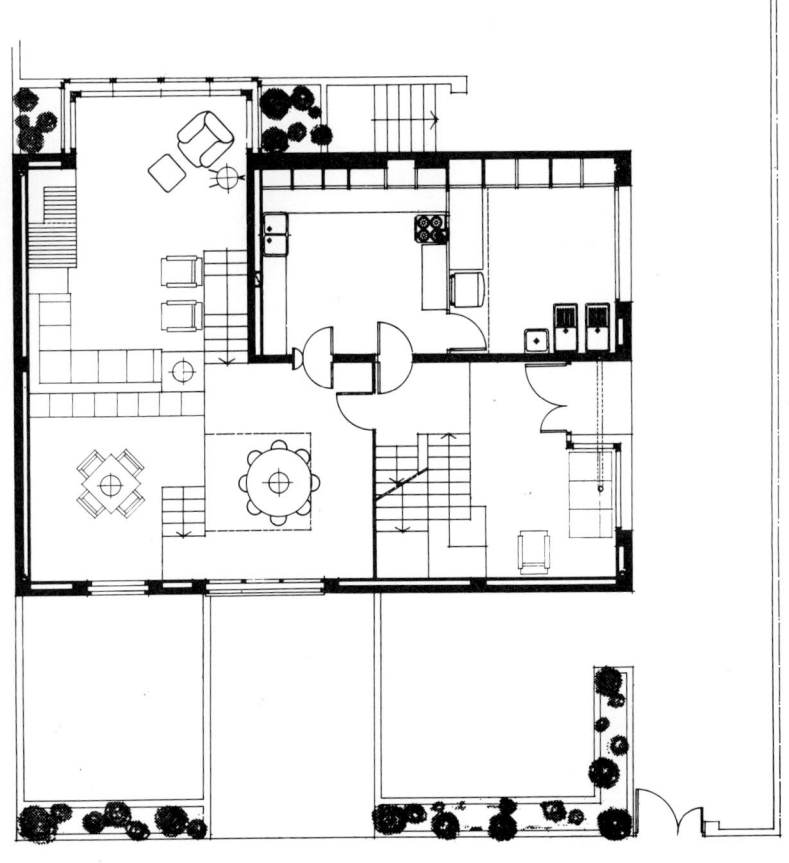

21.3    Plan Scale 1:600

21.4    Section

21.5 The N façade with the garage ramp on the left and main entrance on the right. The debt to Adolf Loos is unmistakable with the simple skin tight cubic treatment of the volume, valuation of the window form as the only decorative effect; the thin coping of the parapet wall and small square punctuations in the recessed upper volume are identical with the Steiner House built in 1910. The lamp cage by the entrance is a reminder of Josef Hoffmann's architectural vocabulary of the same epoch.

21.6 The staircase: The spatial absorption with the entrance hall. (The garage is beyond, and the living room entrance is just visible top right).

21.7 The S and garden façade. The timid, symmetrical arrangement of the combination of the recessed windows with the projecting tribune of the living room below accentuates the major interior element within the composition of the façade.

21.8 The living area. The intermediate compartment containing the card table and library is an off-shoot space from the circulation between the dining and sitting areas. Although this space is vitally incorporated within the whole complex unit it remains isolated, thus the reality of use becomes an element of complexity itself.

21.9 The dining area with the games area below. The surprise discovery of the expanding space as one moves through and down, and turns around is superbly handled.

## 22 CASA PENINA C. Adolfo Agusti, Cardedeu. Province of Barcelona
### 1969
ARCHITECTS: Lluis Clotet, Oscar Tusquets (Studio PER)
CLIENT: Industrialist, wife and three children (2 boys, 1 girl)

### SITE
1.500 m² (1800 yd²) right-angled scalene triangular shaped suburban desert plot with an unpaved access road running along its longest side on the W. Bye-law regulation cut back the building line 3m (10ft) all round. Neighbourhood of poor quality, speculative, vacation housing.

### PLAN
Euclidian composition of triangular enclosing walls parallel with the site boundaries with two enclaves cutting into it from the S. All the walls and divisions follow two directrices of the triangle, the hypotenuse and the shortest side, and the directrix of the median. There is one exception to the rule where the S wall at the extreme end is parallel to the remaining S side of the triangle.

22.1 Plan 1:500

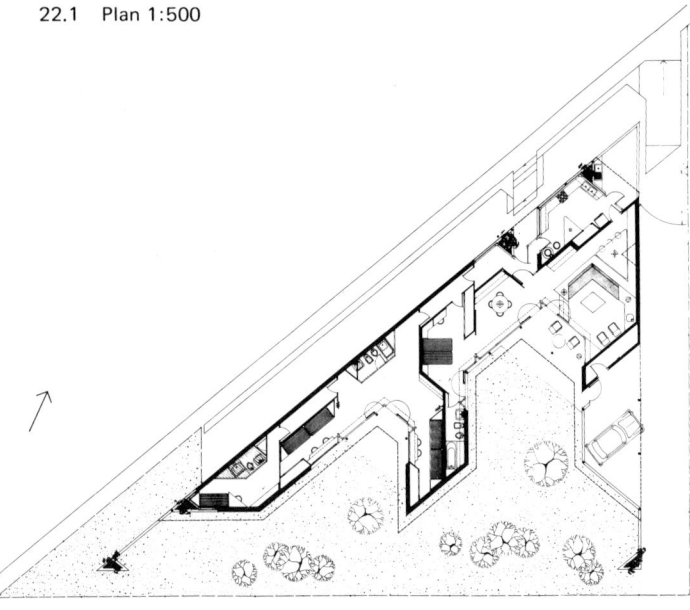

The two enclaves correspond to independent sheltered garden inlets, one for the children with a narrow study-bedroom in each of the prongs joined with a common playroom at the crutch. The other is for the parents, and their entertaining, with the main bedroom suite, card room, living-room gathered around with the screen wall of the car port completing the enclave.

The kitchen and service court within the angle of the two triangular directrices is the only room that has windows directly overlooking the road.

The volumetric form has been obtained by increasing the normal pitch of the 'Catalan' floating flat roof and springing it at right angles from the horizontal cornice that is run along the broken Southern (garden) wall. The geometric projection of the resulting roof planes give an unusual silhouette to the remaining two facades.

### CONSTRUCTION
Load-bearing brick walls, with occasional hollow steel columns, slab roof with an air space covered with an inclined double-flat tile and asphalt leaf on sleeper walls (The Catalan roof).

### AN EXTRACT FROM THE ARCHITECTS INTENTIONS
*"The customer has purchased a tiny lot in a typical area of the most depressing suburbia, without any perspective, completely plain in a rather strange triangular shape (the left-over of a routine plot division), subjected to archaic regulations meant for huge lots, feudal economies, and families in the style of the Lampedusa."*

*"The customer hopes to obtain, or secure, a certain degree of intimacy, sun and contact with nature, by means of an economic construction, easy to clean but above all, really cheap."*

*"If the work produces an unusual or provocative result it is because it attempts to be deeply rational, although unconsciously we may be amused by the scandal which it produces."*

*"Paradoxically a house situated in suburbia does not take advantage of its isolated position and rejects two of its facades (making them completely opaque) which makes it a model house between party walls. In this way it fulfils its function, and it would do so better than in the real circumstances."*

*"It is absurd that a considerable part of the total usable surface of the lot should be completely rejected and even left open to the street which in itself has no value to the house. The plan, which is a filiform or threadlike succession of spaces like a long and labyrinthic corridor, with a facade disproportioned in length to the dwelling area, is not economical, its impression may seem even frivolous and vain. Nevertheless it is the only one we could find in order to make a part of the garden usable, and the dwelling intimate. This was the most logical and beautiful solution we could envisage."*

### OBSERVATIONS
This is the house for Lewis Carroll's Alice, although, according to the architects, Marcuse may have got inside first. The building is no 'obscene merger of aesthetics and reality' neither is it a devaluation of life by a rejection of magic, nor is it the instrument of an alien spirit which makes a game of art. No, this absurd irrational building is the true home of the rational, its unreality is real, its pessimism humorous. Every absurd difficulty, from site to building, from the clients desire for privacy to his distorted pre-vision of it, from an anarchic consumer-bred neighbourhood to a creative sheltered external environment, from generation conflict to dual equality zoning, from the constructive problems of rain shedding to a sculptured volume, have all been dealt with a cultured constructive logic fired with a sense of humour out to shock and surprise. This is the real guts of architecture and Alice would have understood.

22.2 S and garden view of the house. the two enclaves into the triangle create enclosed exterior living areas for children on the left and parents on the right. The arrangement of the volumetric form of the roof can be clearly seen.

22.3 The parents' garden enclave

22.4　The NE façade with the car porch on the left and the small kitchen court on the right. The chimneys and rooflights have been placed against the façade to introduce an incidence of surprise into the logical development of the geometrical roof silhouette.

22.5　The NW road and entrance façade. The house itself forms the effective property limit with the intermediate flange spatially incorporated with the street—a welcome social gesture.

22.6　The living area looking towards the garden and on the right to the card room. The sunken sitting area and adjoining dining area are rather awkwardly handled with the triangular forms getting the upper hand (see plan)

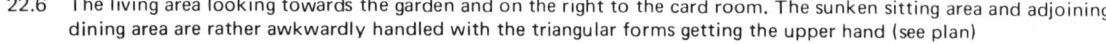

114

22.7 The entrance. The brickwork is both stepped up in scale and
given a horizontal stress with recessed bands that faintly echo
the expressionist work of the Amsterdam school, or Mies
van der Rohe's Rosa Luxemburg monument.

22.8 The play area that joins the two children's
rooms at the crutch of the garden enclave
forming part of the 'umbilical cord' that runs
back into the parents' zone.
The marked lines of the floor tiling clash with
the otherwise harmonic directrices of the house.

22.9 One of the children's study bedrooms.

# INDEX

*Page numbers in italics refer to illustrations or text related to illustrations*